THE ECONOMY OF

YOU

Discover Your Inner Entrepreneur
and Recession-Proof Your Life

KIMBERLY PALMER

AMACOM

American Management Association

New York • Atlanta • Brussels • Chicago • Mexico City • San Francisco
Shanghai • Tokyo • Toronto • Washington, D. C.

Bulk discounts available. For details visit:
www.amacombooks.org/go/specialsales
Or contact special sales:
Phone: 800-250-5308
Email: specialsls@amanet.org
View all the AMACOM titles at:
www.amacombooks.org
American Management Association: www.amanet.org

This publication is designed to provide accurate and authoritative information in regard to the subject matter covered. It is sold with the understanding that the publisher is not engaged in rendering legal, accounting, or other professional service. If legal advice or other expert assistance is required, the services of a competent professional person should be sought.

LIBRARY OF CONGRESS CATALOGING-IN-PUBLICATION DATA
Palmer, Kimberly.
  The economy of you : discover your inner entrepreneur and recession-proof your life / Kimberly Palmer.
      pages cm
  Includes bibliographical references and index.
  ISBN-13: 978-0-8144-3273-0
  ISBN-10: 0-8144-3273-5
  1. Part time self-employment. 2. Entrepreneurship. 3. Small business. I. Title.
  HD5110.P35 2014
  658.1'1—dc23   2013016370

About AMA
American Management Association (www.amanet.org) is a world leader in talent development, advancing the skills of individuals to drive business success. Our mission is to support the goals of individuals and organizations through a complete range of products and services, including classroom and virtual seminars, webcasts, webinars, podcasts, conferences, corporate and government solutions, business books and research. AMA's approach to improving perfor-mance combines experiential learning—learning through doing—with opportuni-ties for ongoing professional growth at every step of one's career journey.

Printing number
10 9 8 7 6 5 4 3 2

Contents

For Kareena and Neal

Acknowledgments

THIS BOOK WOULD NEVER HAVE GOTTEN OFF THE GROUND WITH-
out the generosity of the many side-giggers who shared their experiences with me. I'm so grateful to each of them, for talking with me,
sharing their days with me, and allowing me to tell their stories.

I'm deeply thankful to my colleagues at *U.S. News & World Report*,
especially Kim Castro, for providing such freedom and support to
write about the constantly changing world of personal finance. The
idea for this book grew out of a series of stories on mastering the new
economy that I wrote for *U.S. News*, which is also how I first met many
of the side-giggers mentioned in these pages.

Many researchers, librarians, and fellow reporters also helped me
as I tracked down key data on moonlighting. I especially thank Steve
Hipple at the Bureau of Labor Statistics and Jenny O'Shea at *U.S.
News*, who knows her way around the *Oxford English Dictionary* better
than anybody (and she has the magnifying glass to prove it!).

Ever since first meeting my agent, Melissa Sarver, I've felt lucky to
know such a ceaseless advocate for books and writers. Her ideas,
energy, and help made this book possible. I also thank the wonderful
team at AMACOM, including Irene Majuk, Debbie Posner, and Michael

Sivilli, and especially my editor, William Helms, for believing in this book and providing constant feedback, suggestions, and encouraging Tweets.

My family gives me the love and support that keeps me going—my parents, Chris Palmer and Gail Shearer, have done so since birth, along with my sisters, Jennifer and Christina Palmer. My grandmother, Janet Shearer Johnson, another source of unconditional love, also helped me with my research by sharing news stories on side-gigging with me. My husband, Sujay Davé, has been my best friend and biggest supporter ever since we met, and our children, Kareena and Neal, give me the motivation to keep going—and also excellent reasons to stop and play.

Introduction: Do the Hustle

I REALIZED SOMETHING HAD TO CHANGE AS I WAS DRIVING HOME from work on the way to pick up my daughter from preschool. I had spent much of the day missing her—her giggles, her made-up words, her new attempts at running—and even though I enjoyed my work projects, my mind had frequently wandered. If only I had more control, I thought, I could rearrange my schedule so I worked intensely in the mornings, when I was most creative and productive, and spend afternoons playing dress-up and pretending to be a monkey. Then, I could complete the day's work after her 7 p.m. bedtime.

To make this happen, I needed two things: more power and more money. As flexible as my boss was, she couldn't grant me a half-day schedule without disturbing the well-oiled machine of office life. And I couldn't risk rocking the boat too much because I needed my salary— badly. The sorry state of the journalism industry (and the economy in general) was impossible to ignore; meanwhile, the demands of our mortgage, childcare costs, and college savings weighed on me. Because of those major (and relatively new) responsibilities, I worried constantly about getting laid off; it was one of my frequent nightmares.

The only way to really get what I wanted was to go outside the traditional economy that runs on full-time jobs with set hours. I needed to become financially independent by earning extra money on top of my full-time job, so I was no longer vulnerable to a layoff and could, eventually, work for myself and set my own schedule. It was really about so much more than money. I wanted to be in control of my life.

Soon, I started seeing people on a similar quest everywhere: When my favorite deli down the street from my office closed down, the owner's son ramped up his own custom cake business, which let him keep his customers and replace his income stream. In my own office, I discovered a coworker who was running a social media consultancy, another who ran a print shop, and a third who maintained a productive honeybee farm in his spare time.

Through my work reporting on the economy, I met others who also maintained their side-gigs and full-time jobs alongside each other indefinitely, creating a stable, hybrid income for themselves. Many realized, as I did, that their full-time jobs could disappear at any moment, and they were keenly aware of how devastating that would be. They wanted to protect themselves and their families. A laid-off architect posted a few state-shaped cutting boards she had made for her wedding on the handmade marketplace website Etsy.com, and within months had sold thousands and turned her hobby into a full-time business, giving herself and her family more job security than she ever had as an architect. A bookstore manager, frustrated with her long hours and $28,000 salary, realized she was never going to afford the kind of life she wanted for her family without making a drastic change. So she launched her own entrepreneurial coaching business aimed at creative and crafty types. Within two years, her annual income shot to $150,000, and she gained complete control of her schedule.

These aren't your typical entrepreneurial success stories. Most of us don't even think of ourselves as entrepreneurs, and we didn't start out with the goal of becoming self-employed. (Some of us never plan to leave our full-time gigs.) For the most part, we were forced to invent a new plan for ourselves after the original one began to wobble. These are our stories of survival.

Taken together, they underscore a fact about our economy that few people can afford to ignore any longer: We all need more than one source of income today. Relying solely on a single employer is a sure-fire way to end up struggling, as so many Americans do. Even as the country crept out of its most recent recession, over 8 percent of Americans looking for work still find themselves unable to land jobs. For young people and seniors, the unemployment and underemployment rates are even higher. And those of us lucky enough to hold onto our jobs face pay cuts, benefit reductions, and longer hours, along with the unsettling feeling that those jobs could disappear at any moment. A 2012 Gallup survey found that close to three in ten workers worry they will get laid off, while four in ten fear a reduction in benefits. It's hard to go about our normal lives, picking up groceries and planning vacations, with that kind of anxiety hanging over us.

At the same time, life keeps getting more and more expensive. The prices of food, gas, rent, and even coffee keep going up. Not surprisingly, most Americans report feeling incredibly squeezed financially. The University of Michigan, which conducts the official survey of consumer sentiment, found that in August 2012, half of consumers reported being worse off financially than they were five years before, and the same proportion anticipated no signs of improvement over the next five years. And few have a cushion to fall back on; only one in four Americans have enough money in savings to support themselves for at least six months. News stories are filled with accounts of workers unable to find jobs after layoffs; anyone who continues forward as a traditional worker bee seems destined to end up homeless, poor, and desperate. We can't pretend that our employers have our best interests in mind or even that they will continue being our employers for much longer.

That's why so many of us have decided to look for an alternate way to live. A way that doesn't make us feel like we're balancing on a tight-rope, one misstep away from disaster. We're fighting back against stress and stagnation by pursuing money-earning ventures outside of our full-time jobs (if we still have them). Often, we feel like we have no choice. We need the money, and our primary jobs aren't providing enough of it. Many of us are motivated by an extreme loss, such as a layoff, but just as often we set up shop in anticipation of that seemingly inevitable event. I found more and more people also struggling with my original question—in a world of zero job security and ever-increasing financial pressure, how can we guarantee success for ourselves and our families? The answer became increasingly obvious: We must actively create multiple ways of earning money through entrepreneurial pursuits.

In doing so, we can turn the new economy from a frustrating wasteland of lost opportunities into a thriving incubator for our true selves. Its newest features—the ease of online connections, the intense demand and competition for creative services, the temporary job market—become assets instead of drags. Not only do we improve our financial security, but we often discover we are happier and more satisfied in our new lines of work.

The cultural shift toward a more individualized way of thinking about how we earn money is so profound that even celebrities, television shows, and movies reflect it. In addition to the Hollywood work that makes him famous, Liev Shrieber carved out an additional niche for himself as the go-to voice to narrate HBO documentaries. Gwyneth Paltrow launched a lifestyle newsletter, GOOP, which promotes her brand as well as non-movie products such as cookbooks. Sarah Jessica Parker explained to *Parade* magazine that it was her deep desire for financial security after a cash-strapped childhood that led her to work so hard to capitalize on her fame, and, in fact, it was one of her side-projects, a perfume line, that had turned out to provide much of that financial security in recent years. Just like us, many celebrities want to take back control of their financial fates through entrepreneurial projects, ranging from product lines to websites. While it might seem like they earn huge sums of money, they often make it in chunks and don't know what or when their next job is.

Much of Bravo TV's *Real Housewives*' drama revolves around the women's business ambitions, which is perhaps another reason for the franchise's addictive appeal. We relate to those ambitions. On *The Real Housewives of New Jersey*, Teresa Giudice promotes her cookbooks and other business ventures, while also sharing her attempt to recover from bankruptcy. On the New York version, one housewife hawks white wine while another showcases her branded toaster oven. In fact, much of reality television is driven by the entrepreneurial spirit: *Keeping Up with the Kardashians* (and its related spin-offs), *America's Next Top Model*, *Design Star*, *Project Runway*, and *DC Cupcakes* all revolve around people trying to make their career dreams come true on television. ("We ditched our corporate jobs and followed our dreams to make the world's best cupcakes," says Sophie, one of the stars of *DC Cupcakes*, in the show's opener.)

Bridesmaids, the summer 2011 hit starring Kristen Wiig, zeroes in on the rapidly-downwardly-spiraling life of Wiig's character after her cake shop closes. As she struggles to get back on her feet, she holds down a job in a jewelry shop, and bakes at home late at night. Just as she reunites with her love interest at the end of the movie, the audience is also led to believe she will find her way back to a baking career. 2012's *The Five-Year Engagement*, starring Emily Blunt and Jason Segel, similarly ends with Segel's character finding economic redemption, after a string of low-paying kitchen jobs, by launching his own taco truck. Even 2012's *American Reunion* ends on an entrepreneurial note, with Stiffler, who's been stuck in a dead-end temp job, picking up his first party-planning gig.

It's not that the concept of finding happiness through entrepreneurship is new; Diane Keaton made the same leap in 1987's *Baby Boom* to launch a baby applesauce business, and Tom Cruise's character famously starts his own agency in 1996's *Jerry Maguire*. It's that the reasons are different. In the 1980s, as the number of working moms rose and women struggled to find balance, audiences wanted to watch as Diane Keaton struggled and found the way forward. In the 1990s, as corporate America boomed and people worried about selling their souls in exchange for rewarding paychecks, they wanted to watch Jerry Maguire navigate that maelstrom and come out ahead. And now, as we watch our jobs slip further and further from our grasps, and wonder how long we can rely on our next paycheck, we want to see our movie protagonists and reality television stars do the same, while ultimately finding a way to take back control. In its Index of Entrepreneurial Activity, the Kauffman Foundation reports that entrepreneurial activity is at a fifteen-year high, with the largest share of entrepreneurs under the age of forty-four. According to Google

Insights, which tracks the popularity of different search terms, the number of people Googling the term "entrepreneur" spiked in late 2009 and early 2010, when the economy was at its most sluggish.

The shift has sparked its own language: "Digital nomads" build their side-gigs and "portfolio careers" so they can become location-independent "solopreneurs." They talk about creating their online "tribes" to support them, maximizing their online brands to reach more people, and selling digital products like e-books and guides while they sleep. They blog about waking up to work at 5 a.m. because they are so excited to get going, and then staying up until 1 a.m. to finish a project they can't wait to put out into the world. Many of them do all this before or after heading off to full-time jobs that in some cases aren't even related to their independent ventures. They do it to pursue the dream of financial freedom.

Even Daniel Pink, who first identified the shift toward work independence in his 2001 bestseller, *Free Agent Nation*, says he didn't predict the current explosion in self-employment (including side-gigs), which he attributes both to new technology that makes it easier to work for yourself and to the slack economy. "Employers do not give employees security today," he says.

Reid Hoffman, cofounder of LinkedIn, makes a similar point in his 2012 book, *The Start-Up of You*: "To adapt to the challenges of professional life today, we need to rediscover our entrepreneurial instincts and use them to forge new sorts of careers. Whether you're a lawyer or doctor or teacher or engineer or even a business owner, today you need to also think of yourself as an entrepreneur at the helm of at least one living, growing start-up venture: your career."

Meanwhile, a powerful group of online leaders has risen up to affirm those instincts and get us on the path to self-employment. They are charismatic and persuasive, and their very existence proves that the dream is possible to achieve. One of them, Chris Guillebeau, author of *The Art of Non-Conformity*, constantly urges his thousands of followers to question the need to hold down a full-time job, own a house, and other staples of the traditional economy. He also teaches by example, supporting himself through his blog, book, and digital career guides that sell for $40 and up.

In many ways, holding onto our main jobs as long as we can while slowly building our entrepreneurial projects gives us the best of both worlds: Despite cutbacks, our full-time jobs often still come with health insurance (and possibly disability and life insurance), a steady paycheck, opportunities to develop our skills, socialization, and a help desk. Meanwhile, our side-gigs offer a chance to diversify and increase our income, pursue creative fulfillment, try our hand at running a small business, and exert more control over our work. We get the benefits of both the corporate world and the self-employed one. (Of course, there are downsides to the arrangement, too, the biggest of which is juggling what can feel like two full-time jobs, and we'll talk more about that later.)

Not everyone wants to be self-employed, and voluntarily leaving a job in today's economy can sound as crazy as burning provisions in a famine. Why would anyone walk away from a perfectly good job, even if he doesn't love it, to launch his own venture, when thousands of people are unable to find employment? Many people wouldn't. At the same time, the pull toward free agency is even stronger, because we don't know how long our current jobs will last, and, given social media and smartphones, launching something on the side can be as easy as sending a Tweet. Our entrepreneurial side-gigs offer us a third way, not as scary as full-blown entrepreneurship and not as dull as standard office life.

Given those benefits, it's no wonder 30 percent of the freelancers on Elance.com also maintain full-time jobs. Or that the Bureau of Labor Statistics reports that about over 7 million workers, or around 5 percent of the workforce, hold more than one job. (For those with professional jobs and advanced degrees, the rate is over 7 percent.) In fact, the actual number of side-giggers is probably far higher than the official government data suggest, since the Bureau of Labor Statistics only counts those who say they had "more than one job" last week. Side-giggers who do occasional freelance work, for example, might not answer that question affirmatively.

Indeed, when a 2011 survey by MetLife asked respondents what they were doing to increase their income and financial security, one in four twenty-somethings said they were freelancing, and two in ten said they were working a second job. The numbers were slightly lower but still significant across thirty and forty-somethings as well as baby boomers: 17 percent of Generation X (now in their thirties and forties) said they freelanced to boost their income, and 12 percent of baby boomers (now in their fifties and sixties) said the same. Our side-gigs serve as our shining white knights, ready to save us from the evil dragon of the sluggish economy.

The enthusiasm and excitement of these entrepreneurs, side-giggers, and freelancers is infectious. They prove that building a life outside of the traditional economy isn't only possible, but that it's the new definition of financial success. To address my own financial vulnerability, I decided to join them and launch my own business. I had been writing the occasional freelance article since high school, but I wanted to take my side-gig to the next level, and develop a reliable income outside my full-time job. Inspired by the people I had interviewed, I launched my own line of planners, based around life events and goals: The Baby Planner, the Debt-Free Planner, the Money Planner. Under the banner "Palmer's Planners," I opened my store on Etsy. It was thrilling, empowering, and hard.

As I discovered firsthand, there is a dark side to this movement, too. Its evangelists don't talk about it much, but being entrepreneurial means facing the inevitable setbacks. It takes some degree of blind optimism to market oneself, persuade people to pay you for it, and continue, despite hiccups and even failures. But the payoff for persevering is big: After many bumps, false starts, and surprises, I reached my goal of earning an extra $10,000 outside my regular salary for the year. More than that, I felt free. I stopped worrying so much about whether I was going to get laid off, because I had a parachute ready to carry me to safety if I found myself suddenly ejected from my job. Careers used to be like Boeing 757s, gliding us along steadily at 30,000 feet with nary a bump during take-off and landing. Now, we're all flying our own fighter jets. Bringing along a parachute for the ride should be standard operating procedure.

Almost all of the modern-day side-giggers I interviewed said that their idea started as a small hint in their minds that they thought could turn into their financial safety nets. From the baker who launched his own custom cake business to the bookstore manager who decided she'd be better off launching her own coaching business, these vanguards of the new economy tend to share nine common traits:

1. They know exactly what motivates them, and it often starts with a big loss or other major event in their lives.

2. They choose entrepreneurial pursuits that line up with long-standing passions, interests, and skills.

3. They minimize their expenses in both their professional and personal lives, while finding ways to invest in their venture.

4. They rely heavily on online communities of similarly minded people.

5. They actively and shamelessly promote their brands through social media and other grassroots marketing efforts.

6. They master time management strategies that enable them to maintain full-time jobs along with their side-ventures (and the rest of their lives).

7. They find ways to be resilient in the face of inevitable setbacks.

8. As their businesses grow, they support other small shops and start-ups by outsourcing tasks, which further enhances their own businesses, and often find other ways to give back as well.

9. They derive a deep sense of financial security and fulfillment from their businesses, far beyond money.

Through their stories, this book will teach you how to join them. We'll meet Chris Hardy, an instrument repairman who also has a talent for speaking in cartoon voices. When he offered voiceovers for $5 a pop through the website Fiverr, he soon started picking up a handful of gigs a day. He's since expanded his services and now earns one-third of his pay through his voiceovers. Information technology workers (and married couple) Beena Katekar and Sudhansu Samal built their own budgeting app, partly inspired by their young daughter's questions about what she could buy at the store. The app was soon featured in national magazines, including *Parade*, and they've since sold thousands of copies. Beena and Sudhansu continue to build their app business alongside their full-time information technology jobs. Videographer Calee Lee wrote a children's book after noticing a dearth of female role models in kids' literature; she now runs a thriving publishing business that brings in as much annual income as her first job after college. And Alisha Williams, an Olympic-hopeful in track, continues to pursue her running dream, picking up sponsorships from Adidas and PowerBar, while working full time as a certified public accountant.

This book will help you get your own side-gig ready to launch—to save you from financial fear and frustration, to make you more secure and wealthy, and to give you a sense of satisfaction and personal accomplishment beyond what you get from your main source of employment. You'll be building the economy of you.

CHAPTER

1

Give Me a Reason

WHEN I FIRST MET CHRIS FURIN, HE WAS BEHIND THE COUNTER OF HIS dad's deli in Washington, D.C.'s, Georgetown neighborhood, asking me what I wanted for lunch. He had been working there for twenty-seven years, often seven days a week, and regular customers were used to seeing his friendly smile.

Chris, who at forty-one looks like a more muscular version of actor Chris Klein, wasn't just taking salad and sandwich orders. He was also slowly building a business of his own. As television shows like *Cake Boss* and *Cupcake Wars* took off, customers started calling and asking for personalized concoctions of their own. "Somebody wanted a cake in the shape of the United States. 'It's a pain in the butt,' our chef said, and he'd just say no. I'd say, 'Wait a minute. Our economy is headed down. How can I say no?' So I would say yes. I got the chef to bake the sheet cake and then I would stay late and shape it at night, and charge more money for it," says Chris. "I can make sandwiches for three hours and make $100 or a cake in forty-five minutes and make $300," he says.

He liked his new side-gig. "In the restaurant, I was waiting on people and taking orders, and there wasn't so much baking or decorating.

I'm a creative person; I enjoy doing that." And he's good at it. "I felt like I had some talent. I can draw," says Chris.

As property taxes and food prices rose and his dad struggled to keep the deli afloat, Chris knew he needed to prepare for the day when it would close. "Things were going down; bills were piling up. I went into emergency mode. I started wondering, 'How am I going to survive if I lose my job?'" That's when he got serious about building what he would call Cakes by Chris Furin.

Over the course of two years, Chris perfected his craft in the deli's kitchen after it closed for the day, creating cakes in the shape of Darth Vader, Dr. Seuss, the White House, and a Mercedes Benz. "I wanted to take it up a notch, and I wanted to take my price point up a notch," he says. Thanks to the deli's proximity to the Four Seasons and other high-end hotels in Georgetown, he made cakes for big-name clients, including Joan Rivers and Whoopi Goldberg. He also reached out to managers of local restaurants and hotels, who could make lucrative referrals when clients needed big orders for events, including weddings.

As the deli's closing looked increasingly likely, Chris hired a free-lance web designer to set up his website, and his wife, Dawn, who works in marketing, helped make the site easy to find through web searches. He created a limited liability company through legalzoom.com, ordered brochures and other marketing materials through vistaprint.com, and applied for a local catering license. With Dawn's help, he was also able to capitalize on some of the local press coverage the deli got as it shut down, with some sources, including *The Washington Post*, announcing his new custom cake business. He made sure the deli's now-defunct website pointed customers directly to his own.

On July 31, 2011, when the deli officially shut its doors for good, Chris felt "scared, sad, and happy." He was ready to leave a situation where he had started to feel trapped, but he wasn't sure if he'd be able to replace his income with his cake business. When he said goodbye to the other employees that day, he left with a database of a couple hundred customers, a few leftover mixers and shelves, and the urgent desire to make his own company a success.

When we spoke about his business by phone shortly after the deli closed, Chris invited me to see him at work as he prepared an order out of the kitchen of his home in Rockville, Maryland, just outside of Washington, D.C. His two small, white poodles greeted me at the door, and Chris welcomed me upstairs to his kitchen, where he and Manuel, a former deli employee who now works for Chris a few hours a week, were cleaning up after a morning of baking. "Doing it from home saves five to ten thousand dollars a month in rent," says Chris, whose fingers were stained with red icing. "Plus," he jokes, "my kitchen is a hundred times cleaner than that restaurant ever was." His standard-sized oven isn't large enough for big sheet cakes, so he bakes them in pieces and then glues them together with icing. Huge Tupperware containers of cake mix, flour, and sugar line the floor, and the sun streaming through the orange curtains on the windows highlights smudges left from earlier efforts on the black granite countertops.

Order forms for the week's cakes are lined up on a bulletin board, along with a photo of Joan Rivers showing off her orange and brown Hermés bag–shaped cake and a photo of a pink and white ballerina cake with a billowing dress made out of icing. "A customer wanted a cake for her daughter's birthday, so I Googled and found this princess cake," he says.

That princess cake sits in the basement garage that he converted into an extension of his kitchen. A brown-haired Barbie wrapped in Saran wrap stuck out of the rolled fondant pink and white dress; the four-year-old recipient will get to keep the doll when she's done eating the cake. Also in the fridge: a four-tiered white wedding cake, a red cake featuring the logo of a local company, stacks of Philadelphia cream cheese for icing—and Heineken, for when Chris's day is over. Silver sheet trays from the deli, packets of nuts and sprinkles, and cake boxes are stacked around the room, which also houses Chris's weights and motorcycle, as well as his biggest start-up expense, a $2,500 industrial-size refrigerator.

The dining room next to the kitchen serves as his office, where his laptop, a file full of invoices, and brochures with the Cakes by Chris Furin logo monopolize the table. (His wife Dawn is fine with the fact that his business has taken over their home, Chris says, because she wants him to succeed, too. He also tidies up at the end of every day before she gets home from the office.) He's sold about $1,800 worth of cakes this week, out of which he'll pay between 10 and 15 percent in costs. Sales go up and down; last week he made a record $3,600, and sometimes he doesn't earn half that. It doesn't quite replace his old income from the deli, but it's enough to sustain the business as he works on growing it and picking up more customers. "I would like to make $100,000 this year. We'll see," he says. He plans to expand from there. Possibilities include launching a mail-order cookie business, ramping up his referrals for bigger orders, and creating even higher-end cakes.

His business not only saved him from financial catastrophe, but it also gave him freedom. No longer tethered to the hours of the deli, he's in control of his schedule now. "I can take on business if I want it, but if I want to take a day off to ride my motorcycle, I can do that, too," he says.

"No matter what you do, you always need to have a backup plan," says Chris, an avid reader of business books. He asks me what my own backup plan is, and seems glad when I tell him about my freelance work. "As a country, we're not making anything. We just consume. We all need to pick up responsibility and do more," he says. On this Friday afternoon, he loads a cake into his truck and gets ready to do just that.

MOTIVATING FACTORS

When I asked other side-hustlers why they got up at 5 a.m. to work on their blog before their office job started, or why they sacrificed so much of their personal lives in pursuit of their idea, they almost always had a specific story to tell. The Bureau of Labor Statistics reports that Americans who hold more than one job are motivated by the desire to earn more money and meet expenses or pay off debt, as well as the sheer enjoyment of their second job. But that only gives a glimpse of the story. The people I interviewed often pointed to big life changes, such as becoming a parent, or vulnerable moments, such as losing—or fearing losing—their main source of income, as the reason they first pursued their side-gig.

For Joe Cain, a retired New York Police Department captain now living in suburban New York, it was parenthood. He started sidegig.com, a website where retired cops and firefighters advertise their services for everything from legal expertise to handyman work, after noticing that many of his fellow officers supplemented their income with side-jobs. He also knew that some people, including other cops, would prefer to do business with badge-carrying officers. As Joe puts it, "Cops only trust other cops."

His website, which he's been running since 2000, now features posts from thousands of people all across the country. "Cops and firefighters have always had side-gigs," Joe explains, largely because the jobs come with relatively modest salaries and their skills are easily transferable to work in security or contracting. The older generation of policemen, he says, have traditionally used side-gigs to set themselves up for retirement, or to supplement their income while raising families. Today, Joe, forty-eight, finds even more cops and firefighters searching for side-gig work, to help protect themselves from the financial fallout of potential layoffs. "In New Jersey, they're laying off cops like crazy. The public sector does not have the security that it used to," he says.

As a result, Joe says, "Everybody's hustling, trying to make a buck. The old way was to get a job at Con Ed and you're set for life. That mentality is pretty much gone. People are more self-reliant. You have to be."

For Joe, though, the decision to launch his own side-business wasn't about money—at least, not at first. In 1987, when he was working as a foot cop in the Bronx, he started investing in mutual funds, which promptly lost almost all their value. He decided to teach himself about investing so that would never happen again; he signed up for tax and finance classes. Eventually, he became a certified tax specialist and began helping some of his coworkers with their taxes. He enjoyed the work, but as he rose through the ranks of the police department, the time he could spend on it was limited.

As captain, he was always on duty, and his home phone rang even when he was "off." There was endless paperwork and management demands. Then, his son was born on September 11, 2001, joining his then-two-year-old daughter. The long hours combined with the emotional upheaval of September 11 made his decision easy: "I said, 'I could be chief or I could be Daddy.'" He chose the latter.

Within three years, he retired, with ambitions to ramp up his side-gig so it could fully support his family. "I saved some money and spoke to my wife. We said, 'It could be tight for a little while, but let's try it.'" His pension from his service helped.

Now, with his son and daughter on the cusp of their teenage years, his business, Finest Financial Group, is booming with over 1,000 clients. It easily replaces his old income as a captain, and he says his hours are infinitely better. In the summer and other off-season times, he works about three and a half days a week. (During tax season, he puts in between sixty and seventy hours a week for about ten weeks.) His office is a mile away from his house, and Joe says he's never missed a concert, Little League game, or school event. "We're the helicopter parents," he jokes—and he wouldn't want it any other way.

Tara Gentile's story also starts with family. In 2008, she was working at Borders, earning $28,000 a year and working long hours. She had a six-month-old daughter at home, and was desperate to spend more time with her. She started looking into potential career alternatives, and settled on ramping up her online presence and starting a coaching business, focused on creative entrepreneurs. She launched her website in January 2009, and built it up while holding onto her day job, which she eventually left. Within two years, Tara, who lives in Redding, Pennsylvania, was bringing home an annual salary of $150,000.

I managed to catch Tara, who's in her late twenties, on the phone while she was attending BlogHer 2011, a conference that attracts both successful and aspiring female bloggers. I wanted to understand how she went from holding a dead-end retail job to becoming one of the most popular and high-earning leaders in the growing field of creative entrepreneurs.

"Business is a constant evolution of understanding what I do well, what I really like to do, and what people need from me," she says. "My main business is offering small business philosophy, inspiration, and advice, through services as a solo business coach and all sorts of informational products, like e-books on blogging and the art of earning," she explains. Her e-books, in fact, make up about 60 percent of her income, with coaching filling in the remaining 40 percent.

Her own motivation has changed, too. While she started out with the goal of spending more time with her daughter and replacing her old income, she has since decided that it's better for her family to focus on building her income while her husband stays home with their daughter. She also gets deep fulfillment knowing that she's doing work that matters to other people.

That's why she's content now to be traveling so much to speak at events like BlogHer, even though it means being away from her family. As she tells potential clients on her website, "It's not enough to simply create a product, dream up a service, or make an offer. Your work must be aligned with your very core to realize its financial potential. As I continue to align my work with my core spirit, I continue to grow my business, becoming free and financially independent." Her "core spirit," or true passion, is helping other entrepreneurs make their businesses successful. It wasn't working the floor of a bookstore chain.

CAREER INSURANCE

Chicagoan Nicole Crimaldi Emerick started Ms. Career Girl (mscareergirl.com), an advice blog for young college grads like herself, as a creative outlet. She squeezed in time for blogging by waking up at 5 a.m. before her office job at an Internet start-up. She wrote about what she and her friends were experiencing in the job market: uncertainty, the importance of connections, and the rising power of social media. To her, career insurance means having a solid list of contacts you can call on in the event of a layoff as well as multiple revenue streams. "You never know what's going to happen as far as employment goes. So you have to have a little side thing so you have more control," she says.

"In the beginning, I posted every day for the first year," says Nicole, who holds a finance degree from Miami University. At first, she earned no money, but then, as her audience grew, she began receiving paid speaking engagement requests and also posted online advertisements to bring in extra revenue. She soon added workshops, consulting work for local career centers, and networking event planning to her repertoire.

Then, two and a half years after starting her site, she suddenly got laid off. "The minute I got laid off, my first thought was, 'Awesome, now I get to work for myself.' It's been hard over the last couple years not to let it interfere with my day job. I love writing and Tweeting," she says. From that moment on, she committed to earning a steady income from what had previously been more of a hobby.

Shortly after her layoff, she hosted one of her biggest networking events yet, dubbed Ms. Career Girl Connect, in Chicago. Over eighty young women paid $15 each to listen to a panel of five women, including small business owners and the social media manager at Career-Builder.com, talk about getting ahead today. Door prizes included free life coaching sessions and spa certificates, and stylists with trunk shows were on hand to provide fashion advice. "I wanted to cut the awkwardness of networking," she says, and she thinks shopping helps women do just that. She plans to grow event revenue through sponsorships and focus on different themes such as personal finance or home ownership at future panels. She's looking into licensing out her career event concept to other cities.

Without the layoff, Nicole says, she wouldn't have time to develop relationships with clients, market her business, or build her brand. "It's been such a blessing. I used to joke, 'It's going to take me getting fired or laid off to do this full time.' But since I was a little girl, I wanted to work for myself."

At the rate her business is growing, Nicole says, she expects to surpass her old income in a matter of months. Plus, like Tara Gentile, she finds the work more fulfilling than she ever found her former day job. "My business is now all about helping women. It's cool to get paid for that."

For television journalist and entrepreneur Tory Johnson, the path to job-juggling also started with a layoff. At twenty, she landed the position of her dreams working as a network television publicist for NBC. Then, she was suddenly laid off. She moved to Nickelodeon and then to a magazine, but she couldn't shake her own uneasiness about depending on a single paycheck. "I had a permanent scar from the pink slip," she says. So she decided to launch her own company, Women for Hire, an online recruiting and career fair source for women. With two babies at home, she invested $5,000 of her own money and started planning her first career fair at the Manhattan Center. "To me, the riskier assumption was that you could just do a good job and expect a paycheck," she says. "There's nothing like the need to make money to cause you to hustle."

Today, Tory also works as a contributor to ABC's *Good Morning America* and has launched a second enterprise, Spark and Hustle, which organizes conferences for aspiring female entrepreneurs. She attributes the popularity of those conferences, which fill up quickly, to the economy. "It's, 'I lost my job and I can't find another.' Or, 'I'm worried about losing my job.' Or, 'I'm miserable at my job because half the department was downsized and it's a miserable environment.' Or, 'While I'm thrilled to have a paycheck, I don't know how much longer this scene can go on and I want to plan for something more sustainable and fulfilling, while providing the same financial security.' Or, 'I've been a stay-at-home mom, and my husband lost his job and I need to ramp up my contributions to the family's finances.'"

One of the tips Tory passes on to attendees is the importance of knowing why you want to be an entrepreneur.

> You have to be very clear on your motivation. People say, "To make money, or to have more control." . . . I say, "Let's go deeper. Why do you want this money?" For me, it was to protect and insulate my family from ever having to experience the sheer pain that I did from a pink slip. For others, it might be to pay for medical treatment for a family member, or to take pressure off their husband, who's been supporting the family. . . . It's important because the going will get tough, and there will be times when you say, "Wouldn't it be easier to do anything else?" But when

you're so clear on that why and what you're fighting for, then that motivating factor is still going to be there.

That, in fact, pretty much sums up the newest research on the best way to go about achieving your goals. Focusing too much on just how we're going to lose weight or make our new business a success can end up holding us back, because we get frustrated when unexpected obstacles mess with those plans. But focusing instead on the big-picture reason for those goals—the specifics behind financial security or a better family life—actually improves our chances of making them happen. That's what Julia Belyavsky Bayuk, a goal expert and business professor at the University of Delaware, and her colleagues found when they tempted a group of college students with candy for seventy-five cents each after telling half of them to form a savings plan.

The group most likely to blow their budgets on candy were the ones who developed savings plans—not exactly what you'd expect. And students who were primed to think more abstractly, through questions on why they want to save money, were the ones who were most likely to decline the candy and pocket the money instead. Bayuk attributes her findings to the fact that thinking abstractly about our motivations can help us keep an open mind, allowing us to take advantage of opportunities that pop up that weren't in the original plan and deal with unexpected challenges. After all, in real life, specific plans get sabotaged all the time. A client doesn't pay his bill. A new product launch flops. The Internet connection fails when you planned to send emails. If we stay focused on the bigger goal and regroup, then those obstacles don't have to throw us entirely off course.

The lesson, Bayuk explains, is that we can increase our chances of success if we focus on the "why" behind our goals along with the "how." She adds that it's important to remind yourself, "What is my goal?"

For many of us, the goal isn't to eventually work entirely for ourselves, the way Nicole Crimaldi and Tory Johnson did when they got laid off, or like Tara Gentile and Joe Cain did when their side-businesses took off. Our goal is more subtle but equally ambitious: to develop a solid secondary source of income, beyond our main paychecks, so we have some measure of financial security that doesn't depend on the whims of our primary employers. The more specific financial motivations often differ by age: Twenty-somethings who find themselves underpaid, unemployed, or underemployed tend to want a side-gig that allows them to take full advantage of their education and potential. Thirty- and forty-somethings facing stagnant wages want to give their incomes a boost, especially as their household and family responsibilities grow. Forty- and fifty-somethings who've seen their own incomes and assets fall over the last decade want to rebuild their finances before retirement, and sixty-somethings and beyond are frequently focused on funding their golden years amid rising costs.

Across all age groups, secondary income streams from side-gigs can fill the gap between primary incomes and expenses, and make up for the lack of raises or pay cuts. If we do lose our jobs, they can keep us afloat as we search for new ones, as well as allow us to maintain a professional identity, build new skills, and make new contacts.

TOP TAKEAWAYS

✳ Successful side-giggers can often point to a specific reason or motivating factor that drove them to first build their outside pursuit.

✳ Big life changes, such as parenthood or a layoff, frequently inspire a commitment to greater financial security.

✳ Some successful side-giggers opt to leave their full-time jobs when their side-gigs take off; others prefer to balance full-time employment with their side-gigs.

CHAPTER
2

The Master Plan

SHORTLY AFTER I RETURNED TO WORK FROM MATERNITY LEAVE IN the spring of 2010, the economy felt like it was grinding to a halt. A series of never-ending what-ifs started running through my head. What if I lost my job? What if my husband, Sujay, lost his job? What if both happened at the same time? The stakes had never seemed so high. As a twenty-something, child- and mortgage-free reporter, I could pretend that everything would be okay. If I lost my job, I could take an entry- to mid-level position, even with a pay cut, if necessary. But now that I was a mom and a homeowner, I knew that if I lost my job, things would be very, very bad. What if we couldn't pay our mortgage? What if, down the road, we couldn't afford college for our daughter? Or retirement?

Those thoughts sent me into spirals of anxiety in the middle of the night, when I was hardly sleeping anyway due to our daughter's frequent wake-ups. It was a recipe for a jittery, stressful return to work, but it hatched a latent daydream that I had long entertained— to make money outside of my full-time job. For years, I had looked enviously on people who seemed to effortlessly find financial success and fulfillment by selling crocheted scarves on Etsy, or by teaching woodworking on the weekends to clients found through Craigslist.

The concept of earning income from multiple sources seemed like the Holy Grail of financial security to me; I dreamed about finding my multiple streams the way a romantic sixteen-year-old might dream of one day walking down the aisle.

I figured I could start by focusing more on freelance writing, although it required a hefty time investment for relatively meager pay. Also, the influx of laid-off journalists into the marketplace, along with thinning advertising pages in the few print magazines that had managed to continue publishing, meant this freelance work was getting harder to find.

I also wanted to speak more, especially after one author told me that she regularly collected $5,000 speaking engagement fees, which was what allowed her to pay the bills while she spent most of her time on the less-lucrative pursuit of writing. I had received several speaking requests since my personal finance book *Generation Earn* came out, and while none of them came with a $5,000 fee, they did pay something, and I enjoyed connecting with audiences and feeling like I was helping spread the message of financial literacy. If I redesigned my website to feature my speaking and workshop offerings, and perhaps reached out to credit unions and other organizations that might want to host me, perhaps that could eventually turn into a solid income stream.

In the short term, though, I wanted something else—something fun, creative, and potentially profitable, and I had an idea of what it could be. A reader had sent me an email asking if a workbook for my first book was available; she said it would be easier for her to get organized if all of the exercises and to-dos were laid out in one place where she could take notes. Since no workbook currently existed, I figured I could create one, and sell it, perhaps as an e-book through Amazon.com.

Around the same time, I interviewed Amy Stringer-Mowat, a thirty-something former architect with an Etsy shop, for a story on recovering from a layoff. She had lost her job in retail design during the recession and had been working as a freelance architect out of Brooklyn when she created state-shaped cutting boards for her wedding in April 2010. Her design experience meant she knew how to design and manufacture wood products, and she had access to the necessary tools and equipment. After she got married, she posted three of her cutting boards on Etsy. Within two months, she had been interviewed by editors at the *Food Network Magazine* and *Real Simple*, which featured her products in its annual holiday gift guide. "We weren't completely prepared, but since I had past experience with manufacturing on a small scale, we had the space and the machines, and we knew how to order boxes," says Amy. By the end of the year, she had sold over five thousand cutting boards and was earning a six-figure income.

As I was researching her shop before our interview, I found myself drawn to the "paper goods" section on Etsy. Sellers wrote and designed calendars, meal planners, and even party planners, and many of them were sold as PDFs, which meant no shipping was involved. The idea hit me quickly: Instead of a workbook, which sounded too much like homework anyway, I could create money planners and sell them on Etsy as digital files. They would help people get their finances organized and be based around big life events and goals, from having a baby to paying off debt to buying a home.

I quickly flew into execution mode. I drafted my first money planner, which walked readers through my best tips on better budgeting, smarter saving, and savvy spending. The first few pages asked people to reflect on their big money goals and personal definition of financial success. Charts helped them map out their net worth and organize all their accounts and passwords; strategies sprinkled throughout, such as how to create a budget that works and where to park savings to get the best return, were designed to help them make smarter money decisions. Given the emphasis on aesthetics at Etsy, I tried to make the planner as visually appealing as possible. I hired an illustrator to create a turquoise and white cover, and then sprinkled her drawings throughout the text. And I studied up on Etsy, scouring a book on how to make money on the website and learning how others had found success. Clear, enticing copy and beautiful photos appeared to be key. I spent hours choosing and cropping the best images to display.

Within two weeks of conceiving of the idea, my first planner was for sale and my shop, which I dubbed Palmer's Planners, was open for business. I felt a rush every time I logged on to see my visitor stats, which hovered at around ten people a day (and most likely consisted largely of my own family members). Still, creating that storefront gave me an unexpected sense of pride; it felt different from when my magazine stories are published, because even though they have my name on them, they are usually group projects, created by my editors as much as by me. My planners, though, were all me. And I was proud of them.

That sense of pride dimmed only slightly when the first week passed and no orders came in. But luckily, that dry spell was only temporary.

GETTING THE BIG IDEA

Many of the side-giggers I interviewed found their pursuits by simply paying attention to the world around them—a single experience, or combination of experiences, often sparked the idea that turned into a mini-business. Tara Heuser, a thirty-something with an art history degree, based in Washington, D.C., started pet-sitting after a friend asked her to watch her two cats while she was away. After Tara got laid off from her job at a custom framing company she put word out that she was looking for more pet-sitting clients, and she also placed an ad in Craigslist. Now, even though she's back at a full-time office job, she maintains six pet-sitting clients and is looking for more. That cash—she charges around $60 per night to pet sit—supplements her modest income from her nine-to-five job.

Married couple Beena Katekar and Sudhansu Samal, who both hold down information technology jobs outside of Boston, had their aha moment at the grocery store. Their five-year-old daughter kept asking them to buy toys. "We kept saying, 'no, no, no,' and she asked, 'Why not?'" says Beena. To make it easier to say "no" (and to minimize the chances of a mid-aisle meltdown), Beena and Sudhansu wrote a simple program for their iPhones that compared how much their daughter had in her piggy bank to the cost of the toy. If the cost was higher than the amount she had saved, the program denied her request. If she had enough, then it said, "Yes."

It worked so well that Beena and Sudhansu soon began wondering how they could create a "grown-up" version to sell as an app to adults. They ended up designing a program that asks users about savings, expenses, debt, and other factors, as well as the cost of the desired item, and then spits out an answer: approved or denied. The answer comes with an explanation: "You don't have enough savings," or "you need to pay off debt first." Beena and Sudhansu say part of the benefit is simply getting people to look up their own financial numbers.

Soon after making their app, Can I Buy?, available through Apple's App store for $1.99, it was featured as a top money app in *Parade* magazine. Beena and Sudhansu quickly sold over 1,000 copies, and they have plans to expand with more upgrades and features in the works.

Chris Hardy's idea came from a radio talk show. He was a repairman for school band instruments in North Carolina when he heard about Fiverr.com, a website that lets people sell products and services for $5. "I started thinking, 'What can I do for $5?'" he recalls. A former voiceover actor now in his late forties, Chris tried out one of his talents, speaking in cartoon voices. "I will speak your message in a cartoon voice of your choosing," he posted.

Within two weeks, Fiverr featured his offering on the homepage, which led to a burst of sales. Now, he gets up to twenty orders a day and is on track to earn close to $10,000 this year. He spends between two and five hours a day working on his voice recordings and editing them. "I charge $5 for a quick edit, and an extra $5 for a more professional-level edit," he says.

As a result, Chris says, "It seems like a constant stream of money is going into my PayPal account." At first, he used the money to pay for his wife's college costs, including $800 worth of textbooks. Then, he and his wife decided to move to Augusta, Georgia, and his Fiverr income became even more important as he switched to working as an independent contractor for a family-owned music store. "Fiverr is a third of my income right now, and I can set my own hours," he says in his authoritative voice. (Whenever I talk to him, I feel like I'm interrupting the narrator of a movie trailer.)

As Tara, Beena and Sudhansu, and Chris show, choosing a side-gig is deeply personal; the right one fits like a favorite pair of jeans, stretchy in all the right places. Side-giggers find ways to exploit their unique skills and interests along with what's currently marketable. A side-gig offers the chance to return to a childhood hobby or long-abandoned skill. Or it can be the opportunity to quickly pull in cash from a talent that's currently in demand, from voice impersonations to clever Tweets.

If you're reading this book, you might already have a budding idea of what your side-gig could be, or perhaps you've already launched one. But if you're still looking for that initial spark, these kinds of big-picture questions can help jostle loose any latent ideas:

1. What do you read about in your free time, or browse on the web?

2. What topics do you most often discuss or email with friends?

3. What are friends or family members most likely to ask for your advice about?

4. What makes you jealous—any friends' accomplishments, or Facebook posts, that make you think, "I wish I was doing that?"

5. How do you most enjoy helping people?

6. What can only you create?

7. What services do you enjoy providing for free?

8. What do people you consider role models do to find new sources of income?

9. What is easy for you to do that other people find difficult?

10. What part of your full-time job do you most love and wish you could do more of?

Asking friends to answer these questions for you can also shed light on how others perceive you and may open your eyes to side-gig strengths. You might be surprised to hear that they think of you as their go-to party-planning expert, or that you give the best relationship advice. For more ideas and inspiration, you can flip to *The Economy of You* Handbook in the back of the book. The exercises are designed to help generate and launch side-gig ideas, and the list of top fifty side-gigs shows what is currently popular and profitable. (You can also download "Find Your Gig" at economyofyou.com.)

Fishing for Gigs

Websites where other side-giggers advertise their own products and services can help spark the idea for your own venture. Here are some top resources:

Craigslist.org: Its old-school feel also makes the site easy to use; people market skills ranging from tutoring to lawn services.

Elance.com: Creative professionals gather here to offer their marketing, writing, sales, and technical skills.

Etsy.com: This site features handmade and vintage items created by artists and other creative types, with a strong emphasis on visual appeal.

Fiverr.com: Among the quirkier new sites, Fiverr.com makes it easy to sell any product or service for $5.

Freelancer.com: Like Elance.com, this site caters to online professionals, both technical and creative, looking for work.

Guru.com: Projects related to e-commerce, engineering, and design are most popular on this freelance site.

Odesk.com: This site features web development, writing, design, and other online skills.

ON-THE-JOB INSPIRATION

One of the richest sources of side-gig ideas, in fact, might be your day job. Many of the side-giggers I interviewed created their gigs from some variation or offshoot of their full-time career. Maia Heyck-Merlin, senior advisor at Achievement First, an educational nonprofit in New York City, discovered her side-gig after noticing that many of the teachers, principals, and nonprofit managers she works with struggle to stay organized. As someone who's always been naturally well organized, Maia started sharing her tricks with her coworkers. "I would have staff members over and we would spread out papers on the floor," she says. As a former teacher herself, she developed a method of what she calls "togetherness" that was particularly useful to educators, who often have information coming at them all day long from different sources. "When you're behind a desk and have no time for a bathroom break and no time for emails or text messages from parents or messages over the intercom, it's really hard to stay organized," she says.

As Maia, now in her mid-thirties, developed her strategies, more and more teachers started asking for her help. She started giving workshops for teachers and school leaders. A former colleague from Teach for America connected her with education executives interested in one-on-one coaching. Then, a local graduate school, the Relay Graduate School of Education in New York, heard about her work and hired her as an adjunct professor, and she picked up even more clients. She juggles her full-time office job with her company, Brass Tacks, by applying her time management techniques to her own life: She starts her day in the office early, leaves by 4:45 p.m., has family time with her two-year-old daughter and husband until 7 p.m., and then two nights a week gets back on the phone to coach clients or talk with teachers until 9:30 p.m.

While she recently scaled back her Achievement First working hours to 50 percent and might soon downgrade her hours further to help her spend more time on her coaching business and promote her book, *The Together Teacher*, Maia has no plans to give up her job entirely. "I love it. I have no desire to leave," she says. And she's found that her bosses love her side-business, too. "It's helpful for their branding," she says. Her nonprofit gains an employee who's an expert in time management and organization for educators.

Any stress that comes from that balance is well worth the satisfaction she gets from feeling like she's helping teachers do their jobs better. Teachers often tell her, "Thank you, now I think I can do this job for longer," and with so many teachers burning out and leaving the profession, she feels like she's found the perfect intersection of her own skill set and passion with what the world needs.

Field hockey coach Emily Beach, a childhood neighbor of mine, also found inspiration on the job. She first came up with the idea for a field hockey stick that would make it easier to teach players how to dribble with their left hands when she was sitting in a meeting with her boss, planning a youth hockey camp for three-, four-, and five-year-olds. "I was thinking, 'This is going to be a disaster'—I was picturing them not comprehending the idea or just not being strong enough to use their left hand," she says.

While some coaches slide an empty toilet paper roll over sticks to prevent players from controlling them with their right hands, there's no more durable product on the market to impart those skills. So on a piece of scrap paper in that meeting, Emily sketched out her idea for a stick with a rotating grip. Then, that night, she went home and took a hand chisel to an old wooden stick. Over the course of four hours, she wedged out a gap in the stick that would allow her to slide a plastic pipe over it. She had her prototype. "I said, 'I'm not letting this out of the house'—I don't want it to get stolen. The next day, I started contacting people to find an [intellectual property] attorney," she recalls.

As soon as she got the patent approved two years later, in 2009, she started taking her creation, which she named the Dribble Dr., on the road with her. Since her job as a coach requires her to travel to conferences and tournaments, she had a built-in network of potential customers.

Emily soon set up a workspace at her parents' house in suburban Washington, D.C. Tucked away in a back room in their basement, next to wrapping paper and Christmas decorations, about 150 sticks hang from the rafters, waiting for Emily to turn them into Dribble Drs. The real work happens outside, in the garage: Donning sweatpants, long sleeves, goggles, and a mask to protect herself from flying splinters, Emily spends hours leaning over the belt sander, shaving down the wooden sticks so she can slide the piping over top, and then finishes them off with grip tape. The stick supplier she found in Pakistan has already added her Dribble Dr. logo to the sticks for 25 cents each.

Emily, who's now in her early thirties, launched her business while she worked as a field hockey coach at Georgetown University in Washington, D.C., but she soon got a call from the Stevens Institute of Technology in Hoboken, New Jersey, recruiting her to coach the field hockey team. At the job interview, her future employers asked her about her patent. They said they hoped she would talk to the players, many of whom plan to go into engineering or technology fields and dream of creating patented designs themselves, about the legal and business aspects of her design, along with imparting her hockey skills. "It comes up, and I'm always happy to share," she says.

In addition to coaching work, Emily continues to build her company. She's now sold over two hundred sticks for between forty and sixty dollars each, and has had preliminary discussions with some athletic companies about potentially purchasing her patent, which could lead to a big payday.

Maia and Emily show that pursuing a side-gig that's closely related to your full-time work can actually be a boon to your employer, too. Finding a pursuit that makes your employer look good, or teaches you extra skills, such as html coding or public relations, that your employer can then use to its advantage, offers a double payout—earnings from the side-gig as well as increased value at your job. In fact, even the experience of running a side-business itself is a skill employers increasingly look for. A 2012 survey by Generation Y consultancy Millennial Branding found that one in three employers say they now look for entrepreneurship experience when evaluating potential hires. (If your employer doesn't welcome side-gigs as warmly, or your two jobs are in conflict with each other, you can find suggestions on how to handle that in more detail in Chapter 6.)

As Dan Pink observes in *Free Agent Nation*, "Moonlighting, once a way to get fired, now may have become a way to get hired."

Now that we've stirred up some potential ideas to serve as your financial parachute, let's figure out which ones will really be able to open up and whisk you off to the land of financial security.

GETTING REAL

In addition to focusing on what they want to do, successful side-gig-gers also zero in on the flip side of the equation: what people will actually pay them to do. Some side-gig proponents don't like this part of the conversation, because they think if you work hard enough, then anything is possible. To some degree, they might be right. Sell hand-made purses out of cat hair? Sure—in fact, somebody is doing that right now on Etsy. Earn thousands by blogging about your immense pop culture knowledge? The author of *Suri's Burn Book*, a policy consultant by day, is proof that it can work. But paying attention to the market, and what it will realistically support, can make finding side-gig success a whole lot easier.

Solid side-gig ideas—ones that can take you to the next level financially—usually share the following characteristics:

1. They have low start-up costs.

2. They have a large potential upside and are easily scalable.

3. They fit well with full-time work (or at least do not pose a conflict), which usually means they can be done on your own schedule.

4. They take advantage of your own unique creativity and skill set.

5. They are fun to do.

That's why many highly trumpeted but ultimately disappointing ideas don't make the cut, including taking online surveys, working minimum-wage part-time jobs, or viewing online ads for two cents a click.

Instead, successful side-giggers ask: What fields are growing? What does this world need? What problems can I solve? In general, many of the fields with the most job security are the ones that can't be automated or outsourced. One-on-one services, anything involving creativity, or a complex task requiring a highly educated brain tend to be solid bets. If your own passions and skills happen to overlap with any of those in-demand fields, you're in luck.

Research from popular freelance websites, including Elance.com and Freelancer.com, show that demand for creative, online services is booming, as corporations and smaller businesses opt to outsource more work. Freelancers increasingly handle web content creation, design, marketing, social media, and even data analysis. The July 2012 Global Online Employment Report from Elance found that web design postings increased almost six-fold and content writing three-fold over the previous year. That's convenient for side-giggers, because those types of jobs are also easiest to fit in alongside more traditional, full-time careers.

TESTING THE WATERS

Many side-giggers opt to launch a test run before getting too far into the planning process. It's easy to create a product listing online or start a blog and offer services, and taking that step gives you a chance to fine-tune what you want to offer—and lets you see who might buy those products or services. If you're thinking of starting a copyediting business, for example, then you can create a listing on Craigslist.com or another popular listing site to see if anyone bites. If you want to become any kind of coach or other service provider, then you can start your blog or website and clearly describe the services. If you want to start selling your photos online, then you can create an Etsy or Red-Bubble.com account and start uploading your art. In addition to letting you check out your potential client pool, taking this step is also big psychologically: As soon as you open up your virtual shop, you're officially in business!

Finding a side-gig that can bring in significant amounts of cash is often about experimentation in those early stages. Kylie Ofiu, a hairdresser in her late twenties in Sydney, Australia, knew she wanted to supplement her income—in fact, she has big dreams of becoming a millionaire one day. She launched her quest to earn more first with a blog, kylieofiu.com, where she writes about money-saving and money-earning techniques. She started running advertising on the blog, which brought in a small amount of money, and also tried selling things she no longer needed, such as old jeans and old furniture, on eBay. In addition, she tried her hand at freelance writing for companies and affiliate marketing. At the same time, she continued cutting hair.

As Kylie honed some of her techniques, she realized that she had the potential to earn much more by focusing on her professional writing. She landed a book contract to write *365 Ways to Make Money*, which was released in Australia, and that project led to paid speaking gigs. Her blog helped her grow her audience and make connections with potential speaking sponsors, so she invested her time in that, as well. She's now able to support herself and her family (she has two children) primarily through her writing, along with some speaking gigs at blogging conferences. "My blog itself is not my main source of income, but it has given me opportunities to earn that I wouldn't have had otherwise," she says. Still, Kylie says she constantly reviews and updates her earning strategies every few months to see if she should make any adjustments.

Todd Henry also took the baby-step approach, and started what would later become a thriving business, when he launched a podcast on creativity. As the creative director of a nonprofit in Cincinnati, Todd struggled to figure out how best to keep his team of thirty motivated to constantly think up and develop new ideas. So he started talking about that challenge online, through his podcast, The Accidental Creative. On each episode, he explored creativity-boosting ideas, such as eliminating clutter from your desktop, or eating more energizing food. Soon, he had a steady following of fans who downloaded his podcasts from iTunes. (I first heard about the podcast when a college friend, a graphic designer, emailed them to me because she thought they were so useful.)

"I realized people were listening to it, so that raised the stakes," says Todd. He created a companion website, accidentalcreative.com, and started waking up at 5:15 a.m., before his children, to put in two hours of work before heading to his office. As his costs related to podcast and website management started adding up, he looked into how he could monetize his work. First, he created a membership community, so people could pay to get extra content and interact with Todd himself. He also started selling products, including personal idea pads with prompts. Then, companies began asking him to speak to their employees, often about how to increase their own creativity. That last one turned out to be the big winner, and became the main revenue stream for his company. (He has since left his nonprofit to work on The Accidental Creative full time.)

Taking those experimental steps also gives you the chance to see how easily (or not easily) your side-gig idea blends with your full-time job. For some people, especially for those who work in highly technical or regulated fields with strict ethics codes, this can be a minefield. A doctor, for example, cannot, or at least, should not, moonlight as a sales rep for a pharmaceutical company. A federal worker who approves contracts cannot accept money from potential contractors for after-hours services. A software coder for a big company cannot launch a competing product outside of office hours. (In addition to making sure it doesn't conflict with your job, you might also need to make sure the side-gig doesn't conflict with your living arrangements. Certain residential areas, rental units, condo associations, and local governments prohibit residents from pursuing business activities on the premises without permission or a license; a quick check of your contract or bylaws can determine if you need to take any extra steps to keep your gig legal.)

The perception of an ethical lapse can be just as harmful as an actual breach. Suze Orman found herself under heavy criticism when she launched a prepaid debit card and then used her journalism to hawk the benefits of the card. Heather Armstrong, who writes the popular blog Dooce, was famously fired from her full-time job after writing about work on her site, even though she didn't identify the people or company by name. Actress Hilary Swank's reputation took a hit after she collected a big appearance fee from Chechen leader and alleged human rights violator Ramzan Kadyrov. Successful side-giggers usually go out of their way to make sure their side-pursuits don't jeopardize their full-time jobs, which are still, after all, their primary source of income. But fear of crossing a nonexistent line often prevents people from ever finding a way to pursue their side-gig, and that can be an even bigger mistake than making a minor error that requires an apology.

PREPARING TO LAUNCH

When I launched Palmer's Planners on Etsy, my plan was pretty simple: I would create my products, adding more over time, and promote them by reaching out to personal finance bloggers and writers interested in hosting giveaways and guest posts by me. Then, as I slowly grew my lineup of planners, I would look for bigger distribution networks. I dreamed of a national company like the Paper Source or Container Store eventually licensing my products.

When I sold only one planner after two weeks, I started to get a little frustrated. Where were my customers? And why hadn't the Container Store called me yet? It turns out that thinking too big, too quickly is a common mistake that can actually end up thwarting success. BJ Fogg, director of Stanford's Persuasive Technology Lab and an expert on behavior change, says that people often fail to reach their big goals, such as losing weight or becoming rich, because they focus on that abstract outcome instead of the behavior changes required to get there. He recommends breaking goals into smaller ones that are more manageable.

For those of us intent on launching a successful side-gig, that means taking a series of modest steps to get there, which could include:

- ► Purchasing a domain name for your product or service.

- ► Opening up a Twitter account.

- ► Creating a website describing your services.

- ► Calling someone in your field to ask how they became successful.

- ► Reading a blog related to your pursuit.

BJ, in fact, launched his own side-gig based on this premise. Through his website, bjfogg.com, he offers an online program based on spending just three minutes a day on a new habit, such as writing a single sentence in order to become a novelist. With that gradual approach, the new habit can turn into something significant, he says. He spends about half his time at Stanford and half on his outside projects, which includes corporate workshops and group coaching.

In other words, I shouldn't be discouraged that Paper Source hasn't yet contacted me about licensing my planners. According to BJ, I'll have a better chance of meeting my big goal of financial security through my side-gig if I focus instead on the interim goalposts that will take me in the right direction.

So I slowed my pace and came up with a more realistic, step-by-step plan, and one that could fit with my demanding day job, too. Instead of rushing to launch more planners, I focused on promoting the handful already available. That, it turns out, would be a much bigger job than I realized.

TOP TAKEAWAYS

* Side-giggers often find their entrepreneurial pursuit after an experience that turns them on to a particular need or demand in the world.

* Ideas often grow out of skills gained in full-time jobs.

* Successful side-giggers usually spend significant amounts of time honing and testing their ideas.

* Small steps toward building a side-gig can be more productive than big ones.

CHAPTER

3

Banking on It

THE DAY AFTER EMILY BEACH, THE FIELD HOCKEY COACH FROM Chapter 2, stayed up late chiseling away at her rotating hockey stick concept, she refused to show it to anybody except her parents. In fact, she didn't let it leave her house. Instead of celebrating her invention, she focused on finding an intellectual property attorney who could make sure her work was protected.

The father of one of the girls on the team she coached at George-town arranged a call between Emily and a patent attorney, who first explained that filing for a patent would cost between $10,000 and $15,000. "At that point, I was like, 'I can't do that,'" Emily says. Then the father, who was also on the call, stepped in, and asked if the attor-ney could cut her a deal. The lawyer agreed to help Emily for closer to $8,000. Within two years, Emily had her patent, and she started showing off her stick. Without that big expenditure, as painful as it was, that handcrafted prototype might still be sitting, unused, in her parents' garage.

As Emily found, some costs are necessary, but there are often ways to creatively reduce them. Almost everyone I interviewed strug-gled with the tension between investing in their businesses and con-serving cash. Fortunately, there are plenty of ways, from bartering to hiring young freelancers, to keep costs down—which helps keep profits up.

Maximizing those profits is essential, because even people lucky enough not to be immediately concerned about a layoff or how to afford the new baby that's on the way face some degree of financial uncertainty—that's just the nature of living in our current economy. Most Americans are still struggling to recover from the 2000s, which was so tough on middle-class Americans that the Pew Research Center labeled it "the lost decade." For the first time since World War II, income and net worth fell for most Americans, and we're still looking for ways to build it back up again.

For those of us approaching mid-career, there's also the inevitable flattening of income to contend with. According to a Payscale.com analysis of over 1.5 million college graduates, most people stop getting raises in their early forties (for women, thirty-seven is the average age; for men, it's forty-five). PayScale.com lead economist Katie Bardaro explains that's because people generally start rapidly improving their skills and value in their twenties, when they have a lot to learn, and then they max out around age forty. At that point, more years of experience does little to increase one's value to an employer. (Exceptions include lawyers and highly technical jobs.) Jobs can also start to feel somewhat repetitive at that point, which also makes it an ideal time to start something new on the side.

As we get older, the situation only gets more severe. In fact, self-employment might be the only way people in their fifties and sixties can guarantee themselves jobs at all. The Government Accountability Office recently found that during the economic downturn, workers over the age of 55 were more likely to experience long periods of unemployment than their younger colleagues: The median length of unemployment for that age group was 35 weeks in 2011, compared to 26 weeks for younger workers. Those eligible for unemployment might receive up to half of their former salaries during that time, but otherwise, that's two-thirds of the year without regular earnings.

Those trends are depressing, especially when you consider that income will likely stagnate just as our lives get more expensive: People in their thirties, forties, and fifties are often squeezed by family costs, mortgages, helping aging parents, and paying for children's educa-tion. That means we need a second source of income more than ever as we head into middle age—and that's where a side income can save us. And after fifteen or twenty years on the job, many people have also accumulated the skills and contacts that can help launch one.

Successful side-giggers often anticipate the income drop-off early, and get started on their backup plans when they're still in the prime of their main careers. Isabella Rossellini's daughter Elettra Wiede-mann, who works as a model and also holds a master's degree from the London School of Economics, told *New York* magazine, "Models are like athletes: You burn hard and fast." Her master's degree, she explained, "was setting the groundwork for a Plan B if and when the day ever comes when the phone stops ringing with modeling jobs. You can't count on a career like my mom's. That's very rare." That's the same reason Olympic gymnast Dominique Dawes launched a speak-ing career, *General Hospital* actress Laura Wright runs a winery, tennis star Venus Williams started an interior design firm, and her sister Ser-ena created a jewelry and fashion line. And it's why a lot of the side-giggers in this book got started long before they really needed the money.

Jason Malinak got the idea for his successful Etsy shop, where he sells digital products that give tax and bookkeeping advice to other Etsy sellers, from his wife, Katie. In 2007, she started selling hand-made baby clothes and blankets on Etsy. "She wanted to have a job where she could stay home and earn some money," says Jason, thirty-two, who lives in Colorado Springs with Katie and their two young children. At the time, they were trying to save money to make a down payment for their first home. (I came across Jason's story as I was doing market research for my own shop; he was one of the popular Etsy sellers offering digital copies of their creations.)

As Katie's Etsy business grew, Jason, who works as an accoun-tant, started helping her keep track of her orders, revenue, and costs so when it was time to file their taxes, they would have all the paper-work in order. He soon realized that other Etsy sellers had the same questions. So he took the bookkeeping system he created for his wife and made a more user-friendly version. His basic bookkeeping guide features a time tracker, inventory lists, monthly sales spreadsheets, and an annual summary report.

After opening his shop, he started answering questions on the Etsy community forums, which helped spread the word about his products to other sellers. He soon expanded his product line further, into tax guides and specific bookkeeping tools, such as mileage logs. He worked on creating his guides and emailing his PDFs to customers in the early morning or late at night, outside of his job managing the money of a large nonprofit organization. "I consider it all fun," he says, which means it doesn't feel too much like work. He's also selling to a grateful audience: His customer feedback section on Etsy is filled with customers describing how his products help them manage their shops and insisting that the e-books are as useful as meeting with an accountant.

Because his products are digital, he pays virtually zero transaction costs. He learned basic design himself and then had a tech-savvy friend put his images and text into an e-book format. That means all the money he brings in from his now 1,100 sales and counting is pure profit. He and his wife put the money toward their children's college fund as well as remodeling their house. "It adds to our financial cushion," Jason says. And it doesn't take thousands to create that cushion—during one recent month, his shop brought in around $200. The possibilities, though, go well beyond that. He recently wrote a book about Etsy bookkeeping and plans to launch a related website with even more bookkeeping products.

Febe Hernandez, a federal worker by day, launched a jewelry business to help carry her into retirement. Like Jason, she doesn't yet rely on the income. The twenty-year veteran of a three-letter agency in Washington, D.C. (her agency asked that she not identify it by name), got together with a group of girlfriends for a beading party in 2010, and she fell in love with the craft. "I was overwhelmed with a desire to create, then a few months later I had several dozen pieces, and I had a show," she says. She registered her company as Designs by Febe, got clearance from her agency to proceed, and sold $2,000 worth of jewelry at her first event.

Febe, now sixty, quickly ramped up her business by working on the weekends and evenings. The next year, she held half a dozen shows in New York. She connected with the wedding industry in the city and showcased her wares to brides, who loved her sparkly pearl and gemstone designs. Her business recently started turning a profit, and she plans to continue growing even more once she retires from her agency in five to seven years. In fact, she dreams of opening storefronts in New York, Washington, D.C., and Los Angeles.

KEEPING START-UP COSTS LOW

Calee Lee, a videographer now in her early thirties, found that her side-business brainchild—a line of digital children's books—could be done with very low start-up costs if she used a royalty-only model to pay writers and illustrators and made use of the expensive software she already had for her videographer job to create the books.

She first got her idea after reading an article about Amanda Hocking, the author who sold over a million copies of her self-published vampire books. Around the same time, Calee had started reading children's books to her five- and two-year-olds on her Kindle, but she was disappointed with the quality. Classic books like *The Velveteen Rabbit* just didn't look good: The formatting didn't seem quite right, and the normally vibrant colors of the illustrations went black and white on the screen. "I said, 'I can do better than this,'" recalls Calee. So one afternoon when her children were out and she finished up work early, she started writing a story that she'd been thinking about since a family vacation to Cyprus.

A few years earlier, the family had taken a trip to the Mediterranean island. As they visited monasteries, they noticed that cats were everywhere. After asking around, Calee learned that over a millennium ago, Queen Helena, mother of Constantine the Great, had stopped by Cyprus on her trip back from visiting the Holy Land, and noticed that people were unable to worship because of a rampant snake infestation. She was so disturbed by that state of affairs that she decided to remedy it by sending a shipload of cats to the island to control the snakes. Today, says Calee, those cats are still called "Queen Helena cats." "I thought it was a great story for kids," she says.

Calee also wanted to create more appealing role models than the Disney princesses so popular in children's culture today. "I wanted to give my daughter some princess alternatives and show her beautiful women that were strong in a different way," she says. Queen Helena traveled halfway around the world to help a village in a tangible way. Another one of her protagonists, an English princess named Audrey, gave up her wealth to help feed a village.

Once Calee wrote her first book about Queen Helena, she found an illustrator and put together a contract that established payment to the illustrator through royalties, instead of upfront. That means the illustrator would earn a lot if the book sells well, but almost nothing if it doesn't. "If one of our illustrators works with a big publisher, like Scholastic, they get a very small percentage of proceeds. We offer a lot more." As she invited other authors to write books for her newly minted publishing house, Xist Publishing, she applied the same royalty model to them. Thanks to the success of the books, Calee says many of the contributors are making more money than they would under the traditional model.

To keep other costs down, she asks lawyer friends to review contracts and works out of her home. She already had the software from her videography business that she uses to create the e-books, as well. To save on marketing costs, she launches blog tours for authors instead of paying for advertising.

Today, Xist has over eighty titles and is profitable. Her revenue comes from book sales, largely over Amazon, as well as book rental income. Since most of her titles are part of the Kindle Lending Library, anyone with an Amazon Prime membership can borrow one book for free each month, and Amazon pays Xist for those rentals.

That extra income makes Calee feel more financially secure. "I'm making more doing this than I did as a copywriter when I first got out of school," she says, and in one or two years, she thinks it will exceed her income from her full-time job as a videographer. Says Calee, "It's really nice to go to Target and to come home and see I've made money without doing anything, and to see the people I'm working with have made money, too."

The low start-up costs of Douglas Lee Miller's side-gig also means that he can keep almost all the revenue, instead of using it to pay off expenses. Doug is the kind of person that people often turn to for advice. They ask him, the new media manager at DePaul University in Chicago, how to set up a Twitter account, or how to promote their small businesses through Facebook, or how to train their employees to be social media–savvy. Doug, now in his late thirties, got so many requests for help that he realized that in order to protect his time, he needed to start charging people for it. That's when he launched his social media consulting business, The dbMill, which he now runs in addition to maintaining his full-time job.

His motivation was largely financial: After his daughter was born in 2009, his wife took a break from her work as a costume designer, and the family needed some extra income to compensate for that. "While she was out caring for our newborn daughter, I'd been getting a lot of requests and helping people out a lot, so then I set up a more formal way to do that." Clients came easily since he already had a portfolio to show off and had established his reputation as a social media expert.

Doug found that as someone selling a service—social media consulting—he could get started for almost nothing. Instead of investing in fancy software, he used free Google tools, including Google Drive, which lets him save work and share it with clients, and Google Calendar to schedule meetings. He does much of his work on his iPad while commuting to his full-time job, as well as before bed or first thing in the morning. He puts between fifteen and thirty-five hours a week into his side-business that way. (DePaul, he says, embraces his extracurricular activities, as long as his work for them doesn't fall by the wayside. Sometimes he takes a vacation day or makes up hours outside the typical nine-to-five schedule.)

"I have my head in a device every hour of the day, but I don't mind because I'm doing stuff that's interesting to me and helping people," says Doug. He does have to make sure he unplugs to spend time with his two children, though. "But at the same time, what I do is for them, so they can have stuff," he adds.

Doug also invested $100 for an annual membership in Social Media Club Chicago, a networking group that connects him to potential clients. Those connections have led to presentations at businesses or for individuals on how to use social media to advance their brands or land a dream job.

Those minimal start-up costs mean that his earnings are almost all profit—money that supports his family's daily expenses. As his wife takes on more clients in her costume design work, then he might start funneling the money into college education savings or retirement accounts, says Doug. "For now, it's helping us have freedom to do the kinds of things we want to do. We're spending it on normal operating expenses rather than saving it," he adds.

Calee and Doug used personal connections and relationships, free online tools, and their own digital and web skills to launch their side-businesses on shoestring budgets. And while it might seem like a challenge to keep costs so low, it's actually a good challenge to have, and increases the chances of success. That's because a strict budget—or no budget—at the beginning forces you to invest only in the things that are truly necessary, which not only eliminates distractions but also makes it easier to be profitable more quickly. It also makes it easier to shift gears and try something new if the first attempts to sell a product or service don't go anywhere.

Blake Mycoskie, the founder of TOMS shoes, attributes his shoe company's success to his early frugality. In his book, *Start Something That Matters,* he describes how he started out with 250 pairs of shoes in three duffel bags in his small apartment. His lack of resources, he says, inspired creativity that gave him a competitive edge. TOMS, in fact, started out as a side-project, while he was employed at a different company. "If you have little money and have to bootstrap and improvise to pull things together, that becomes embedded in your company's DNA forever—so as you scale up, you maintain the frugality and efficiency that helped you survive your earliest days," he writes. He points out that Kenneth Cole started out by showing off his shoes from the trunk of his car and Ben and Jerry launched their eponymous ice cream company with just $8,000 in savings and a $4,000 loan.

Adam Baker, founder of the hugely popular Man Vs. Debt blog, which now supports his family, spent just $74 to buy the domain name for his site and a friend's graphic design services. He started blogging about how he was simplifying his life and paying off debt, and now he runs courses, sells digital guides, and speaks about living more frugally. That $74 investment, he says, changed his life. (And it was a good thing he didn't spend much on his domain name, because his original choice, SlowSimpleWealth.com, never took off.)

My own start-up costs were limited largely to the illustrator's services. I found her through one of my favorite "mommy bloggers," who had a gorgeous blog banner that was similar in style to the way I wanted my planners to look: fun, whimsical, and modern. So I clicked through to the credit link at the bottom of her banner and discovered a link to the illustrator's site. As soon as I saw her portfolio of greeting cards, wall art, and website designs, I knew that I had to work with her. She used bright, clean colors and had dozens of clients all around the web. She charged $35 an hour, payable through PayPal, and my planner cover ran me about $100.

If you happen to have $10,000 or $20,000 that you're prepared to put into your business, then it would be easy to spend $5,000 on marketing, another $5,000 on a professional e-commerce website, and $5,000 on supplies before even getting your concept out into the world to see if there is a market for it. But as side-giggers showed me over and over again, there's no need to spend big before you start earning: The Internet makes it easy to quickly design something or describe a service that you offer, and to post it—on your own blog, a site like Etsy, or Craigslist. Getting it out there, for as little money as possible, as soon as possible, while continuing to tweak, update, and improve it, can help beginning side-giggers avoid costly losses early on.

Start-Up Costs:
Spend on This, Save on That

Spending as little as possible before launching your side-gig is a good goal, but some investments might be worthwhile. These questions will help you decide where to put your money:

► **What is absolutely necessary to have in place before launch?** If you need a website, or a cover design for a digital product, and you don't know how to create those things yourself, then consider outsourcing the task to a trained professional. (Not without shopping around first and getting the best deal, of course.) Other investments, such as a social media coach to boost your Twitter skills, can come later, after you've started bringing in money.

► **What friends and family can help?** If you happen to have a lawyer, graphic designer, or computer programmer in the family, then they might be able to assist you for little or no paid compensation.

► **What resources do you already have access to?** Perhaps you have Photoshop on your computer already, or wood-cutting tools in your garage. If your side-gig overlaps with your career or preexisting hobby, then you have a better chance of already having some of the supplies that you need.

► **What skills could you trade in exchange for the services you need?** Bartering is back in these days, especially because finding people through blogs or Twitter accounts is so easy. If you know how to send a media pitch, then perhaps you can do that for a graphic designer in exchange for a professional website header design.

► **What websites can help you get deals?** The website 99designs.com makes it easy (and cheap) to launch contests for designers to create your website widget or book cover. Freelancer.com, Odesk.com, and similar sites allow users to outsource tasks, such as copyediting or managing a Twitter account, for a low cost. (These sites have also been the target of criticism from freelancers who say the format unfairly lowers their prices; you can weigh those ethical concerns yourself and decide if you'd rather pay more to go through a traditional arrangement or cut costs through one of these new sites.)

► **What online tools can you take advantage of?** Blogspot, WordPress, Mavenlink (for project management), Facebook, Google products (Drive, Calendar), Doodle.com (for scheduling), Evernote (for recording ideas), Mint.com (for tracking finances)—the number of free or almost free tools has exploded, and can often take the place of expensive software or service providers.

► **What legal protections, if any, do you need to have in place?** Whether it's by forming a limited liability company or taking out liability insurance (or both), protecting your financial stability is important. For as little as $200 a year, insurers often provide up to $1 million worth of liability coverage, which can pay for legal fees and settlements for some types of lawsuits. Forming a limited liability company is more expensive and time-consuming, but it can offer more protection, especially to small business owners who want to protect their personal assets from any risks they're taking in their entrepreneurial pursuits. Gauge your own comfort level and the risks of your business to decide what kind of protection you need, and consider consulting a lawyer if you're unsure.

► **How can you easily sell your products or services?** Etsy, Fiverr, PayPal, and E-Junkie are just a few of the easy and low-cost methods of putting your goods on the market, without any need for a pricey, self-hosted e-commerce site.

GETTING IN GEAR

Many of the successful side-giggers I met also spent months or even years unloading debt, building up savings, and getting in better financial shape as they prepared to launch their side-businesses. Doing so meant they had more freedom to invest a couple hundred dollars (or more) into their idea, and it also meant that failure wouldn't bring financial catastrophe, because they had savings and other income (from full-time jobs) solidly in place. In fact, knowing that they wanted to make their side-businesses successful is often what motivated better financial habits in the rest of their lives.

Jenny Blake started her blog, Life After College, while she was working full time at Google providing career development and training for employees. As a certified life coach and twenty-something herself, she wanted to share what she'd learned about making mistakes, following big dreams, and celebrating success along the way. She soon realized that her own big dream was turning her blog into a book, which she did in 2011. To make the book launch a success, she decided to take a three-month sabbatical from her full-time job, which meant giving up three months' worth of pay. That investment was worth it to her. "I felt like it wasn't fair to either project if I tried to do both at the same time," she says.

To prepare for that financial hit, she took a close look at her expenses. She realized her restaurant habit was costing her $100 to $200 a week, so she started eating at home more. She created a separate savings account dedicated to funding her sabbatical, and kept to a stricter budget with the help of spreadsheets in Google Documents.

To supplement that savings account, Jenny started looking for other ways to bring in more income, too. She sublet her condo while traveling to promote her book and took on a handful of paid speaking gigs as well as some new life coaching clients. Once a month, she scheduled a check-in with herself to revaluate her budget and decide on any other changes. In the end, she decided the trade-offs were worth the inconvenience. She says, "I wanted to enjoy the time and make the most of it, so that meant enjoying some expensive meals, but I gave up my condo. So I didn't have the comfort of my own bed, but I could spend more on social events, outings with friends, and travel." (Soon after taking her sabbatical, Jenny decided to embrace self-employment as a life coach, speaker, and writer. She left Google for good and moved to New York City.)

Other side-giggers told similar stories of start-up frugality: Chris Furin, the cake designer, started saving up money as soon as he knew Furin's would eventually close and he'd need to go out on his own. He lowered his bills where he could and paid cash for all of his purchases, including his big fridge. Todd Henry, founder of The Accidental Creative, made sure he had multiple clients and sources of income, as well as a hefty savings account that could support his family for at least two years, before going full time with his company. While he was still running accidentalcreative.com on the side, he put almost all of his earnings into savings and avoided treating it like personal income.

Even seemingly wealthy small business owners, like Katherine Kallinis and Sophie LaMontagne, founders of Georgetown Cupcakes and stars of the TLC show *DC Cupcakes*, tell stories of strict frugality in their early days. I first met Katherine and Sophie when we appeared on a local news program on the same day; they came to the set bearing dozens of perfectly glazed cupcakes in flavors like chocolate mint and lava fudge. Soon after, I interviewed them about how they left their high-paying corporate jobs to start their cupcake shop.

Katherine and Sophie originally started as side-giggers, too, tweaking their recipes and honing their products on weekends and evenings while maintaining their corporate gigs (in fashion and venture capital, respectively). They cut their living costs; Katherine gave up her own home and started sleeping on Sophie's couch. Even buying a $50 poster at Kinko's turned into a point of contention. "My husband was screaming at me, 'We don't have $50 to spend on a poster!'" recalls Sophie. "We were painting the walls ourselves and doing a lot of work we should have hired professionals to do, but we couldn't afford it," she says.

The recurring theme, of course, is a sense of modern frugality, which means ignoring all of the loud cultural messages about what we should be buying, whether it's a fancy wedding or big house or a new outfit for spring, and listening instead to our own personal preferences that will lead us to our bigger dreams. Katherine Kallinis was happier giving up her own bed if it meant she could open up a cupcake shop; Jenny Blake similarly traded her familiar pillow for a life of adventure. These successful side-giggers didn't just spend on autopilot—they reworked their lifestyles to reflect their true goals.

Money Check-Up

Before launching a side-gig (or making any other major life change, for that matter), it can help to first give yourself a financial assessment. Here's a guide to getting on top of your money. (You can also download the "Make Your Money Work" template from economyofyou.com.)

► **Where is your money going right now?** Free online tools, such as Mint.com, make it easy to track where money is going and to set up specific savings and budgeting goals. Big costs, including housing, transportation, and food, belong in that analysis, too. Downsizing to a smaller apartment, sticking with public transportation, and eating at home more can make it easier to ramp up savings to fund a dream. Of course, those first two strategies work best if you live in an urban area with easy access to public transportation, and even then, fares tend to go up regularly. All you can do is minimize those basic costs as much as possible, and then compensate for the ever-increasing cost of living by managing the money you have as smartly as possible—and by earning more.

► **Are you carrying any debt?** If you're paying off credit card debt, car loans, or student loans, now is the time to try to unload some of that, or at least come up with a plan for doing so in the near future. The interest payments and fees that often accompany those payments can mean you end up paying much more than the actual value of the loan.

► **Where are your savings?** An emergency savings account of at least three months' worth of expenses offers protection from unexpected job loss, health care expenses, and other costs. Creating one should be a top priority. Additional savings can go towards bigger goals, including side-gig funding. (Of course, if you're married or in a relationship, you'll want to make sure your partner is on board, too.)

► **Do you have a retirement account?** If you haven't yet started putting money away for retirement, consider doing so as soon as possible. The earlier you start, the more you'll have—and the more you'll benefit from compounding interest over time. Retirement accounts such as 401(k)s and Roth IRAs also come with tax advantages, and if you work for a company that matches contributions, you'll add to your retirement fund even more quickly.

► **Do you know where your money is?** Now is also the time to get organized, since the paperwork only gets more complicated once you're running a side-gig. Receipts, revenue, tax deductions, contracts—keeping it all sorted out requires a dedicated folder or binder system to keep track of those documents. Apps and websites, such as lemon.com, expensify.com, and shoeboxed.com, make it easy to put as much as possible online, saved in digital formats. Otherwise, when it's time to file your taxes, you'll be scrambling, and could easily end up overpaying Uncle Sam if you lose expense receipts.

With your finances in order, it's easier to focus on the fun part—the revenue.

RAKING IN THE DOUGH

Deciding how to spend (or save) that new revenue can be as much of a challenge as generating it in the first place. The side-giggers I met often avoided depending on their new income, instead ignoring the money, or spending it only on growing their companies. Then, when their revenue turned into something they could count on, it felt like finding a chocolate coconut frosted cupcake on a cold, rainy afternoon.

Maia, the teacher-turned-organizational guru, says she "pretended the money didn't exist" for the first four years of her business. Only then, she says, as she prepared to scale back her full-time job in favor of more one-on-one coaching, did she invest in a professional photographer, intellectual property attorney, and website designer for her company. Jason, the tax expert on Etsy, uses his earnings to help save for big goals, like his children's future college tuitions. Amanda Williams, creator of the travel blog A Dangerous Business, uses earnings from the cruise and airline advertisements on her site to fund her travels. Kelsey Freeman, a freelance designer, photographer, and substitute teacher, sells her photos on SmugMug.com to pay for Christmas presents for family and friends.

Morgan Hoth, a retired special needs teacher now in her mid-sixties, spends her days creating one-of-a-kind silk scarves and neckties in her studio in her house in Richmond, Virginia. Her hobby-turned-business funds trips, new sofas, and financial assistance for friends in need. "In the summers when I was teaching, I was weaving rugs, dying them, and always playing around," she says. Then, when she got close to retirement, she decided she wanted to get more serious about her art, so she put her creations online through Etsy. She quickly built a steady stream of sales. "I just need to sell one or two pieces a week to be happy," she says. Her scarves, which are painted in bold chartreuse, greens, and purples and often incorporate elements of nature such as leaves or flowers, range from $45 to $200.

Thanks to those sales, says Morgan, "If I want a Temper-Pedic mattress I can have one; if I want to fly to Europe, I can do it; if I want to go on a road trip, I can afford it; if I have a friend hanging at the end of a cliff, I can help." Otherwise, she probably would not do those things, given the "crappy little pensions," as she puts it, that she and her husband live off of. "It gives me the freedom to do things I wouldn't normally do—things that make me happy. I thought going to Europe was for rich people, but I went, and I used my money. I wouldn't have done that otherwise," she says.

More Money, More Taxes

Of course, when you earn more money, you also pay more taxes, and earning income outside a full-time job often means that taxes aren't automatically deducted. You do want to deduct as many expenses from your earnings as possible, because that will help reduce your tax bill, but people often run into trouble with their expenses—usually because they try to deduct too much. Here's an overview of what you need to know:

► **Business or hobby?** The IRS makes a distinction between hobbies and businesses, and it's an important one as far as taxes are concerned. If you're creating scarves or baking bread primarily for fun, not profit, then you can't deduct your expenses from other sources of income. In fact, you could get in a lot of trouble for doing so. In order to legally subtract your expenses from your revenue, the "time and effort" that you put into your activity must suggest that you intend to make a profit and that you can reasonably expect to make a profit in the future. If that kind of sentence already has you wrinkling your eyebrows, then you might want to enlist the support of an accountant who knows the rules as well as his pocket calculator.

► **Defining the home office.** Another hot area for side-giggers is the home office. It's very tempting to convince yourself that you can claim all or part of your home mortgage or rent as a business expense because you are now running a freelance blogging business from your basement. But that's the kind of logic that lands people in jail, or at least across the table from an unhappy IRS rep. In order to legally deduct home office expenses from a mortgage or rent, that home office must be used regularly and exclusively for work only—the space can't double as your playroom or dining area. Similarly, you can't write off the entire cost of the car that you use to deliver your baked goods if you also use that car to drive your children around. Instead, you have to carefully track how much you use the car for legitimate business purposes.

► **Giving Uncle Sam his fair share.** The extra income a side-gig brings in is also taxable, and if you're not sharing your proceeds with the IRS throughout the year, then you can get surprised with a big bill (and penalties) in April. Many side-giggers, including myself, write a check to the IRS every quarter to stay on top of those payments. Again, unless you're a math whiz, this is where the services of a trusty accountant can be well worth the price.

Sydney Owen, a former corporate public relations guru-turned-skydiving marketer now in her late twenties, also opts to direct her side-gig earnings as a career coach into her "fun money" fund. For years, Sydney worked her way up the ladder of a corporate public relations agency in Chicago, and she pursued her real passion on her days off: jumping out of airplanes. But she soon wanted it to be a bigger part of her life than just a weekend hobby. She decided to quit her job and become a skydiving instructor, despite the fact that she was on the "fast track to corporate success," as she puts it.

Sydney didn't want to leave the world of public relations completely; she formed her own limited liability company, which she calls 3Ring Media, and started taking on clients. The Chicagoland Skydiving Center, where she also jumped out of planes, was her first one. Soon, she moved to southern California, where the skydiving season continues year-round, and landed a job as a full-time events coordinator at the Drop Zone, a skydiving center in Lake Elsinore. "I'm putting together awesome events, making sure everyone has a great time," she explains.

While she earns a base salary, it's relatively low, because her compensation package includes free jumps, which she needs because she's training to compete in four-way formation diving, which involves performing a series of formations with teammates while falling toward the Earth. To supplement that income, she took on more clients, including small businesses who want to ramp up their social media presence. She also started coaching people on improving their resumes and fine-tuning their career goals, skills she picked up in college. She mentors college-age students and twenty-somethings in their first and second jobs, to help them "get ready for their next big gig," she says. Sydney schedules client calls on her days off, Tuesdays and Wednesdays, or after work and during her lunch break.

Because her start-up costs were so low (she formed her limited liability company using Legal Zoom, where packages start at $99) and she just needs her phone and an Internet connection to do her job, she can pour her earnings back into her passion. She often funds her additional skydiving training costs that aren't covered by sponsorships. (While her employer covers her jumps, she still has to pay for coaching, supplies, and time in a training wind tunnel that simulates free-fall conditions and allows skydivers to practice their moves.)

Her side-business also buys her peace of mind: "If it came down to it, I could support myself with 3Ring Media, I know 100 percent. It just depends how much time I want to put into it," she says. In a photo snapped of Sydney skydiving, she's so high that the photo captures the Earth's curvature along the Pacific Coast. She looks self-assured, relaxed, focused—and completely confident that her parachute will open and glide her to a safe landing.

Many side-giggers put their earnings into retirement itself, through long-term investment accounts. Since most of us are saving far too little for retirement, and find little room in our budgets to put 10 to 20 percent of our regular salary into retirement accounts as we should be doing, side-gig income can be the factor that allows us to save something for those later years. In *Free Agent Nation*, Dan Pink argues that we'll all be working in some form during retirement, given that we can expect to live longer and be healthier than many in our parents' and grandparents' generations. Getting started long before retirement, both leveraging the resources from our full-time jobs and giving our side-gigs a chance to grow before we really need them, can also lead to a steady stream of income after we leave the traditional working world.

Martie Maguire and Emily Robison, the two Dixie Chicks who launched a separate group, The Court Yard Hounds, on the side, told *Entertainment Weekly* that part of their goal was to build a backup plan for when "the Chicks aren't happening." Martie Maguire explained that she wanted "the security of knowing there's something we can always do. Almost like a retirement plan." Her sister Emily Robison added, "This is our 401(k)."

Along with all of those important financial goals, there was often something even bigger than money driving many of the side-entrepreneurs that I came across, and it got at the core of how they defined themselves. Perhaps because we've seen so many of our parents crushed when a layoff ended a long career and resulted in soul-searching about identities that had been so wrapped up in work, or because we know that we're about as likely to hold onto our jobs until retirement as we are to win the lottery, we resist defining ourselves solely through our primary employer. We want our identities and sense of self-worth to go beyond our job titles. That's why we maintain personal email addresses and social media accounts, personal websites, and personal side-gigs. We are not our jobs, because we know our jobs could disappear in an instant.

And while the amount side-giggers earn often grows and builds over time, it can seem so small at first that many people I interviewed were somewhat embarrassed to tell me how much they earned, even dismissing their efforts as a "hobby," something I found myself doing when describing Palmer's Planners to friends. If I called it a small business, then it sounded like I should be pulling in a couple thousand dollars a month, or at least a few hundred on a regular basis. But what I quickly learned as I spoke to more people undertaking similar quests was that it wasn't the size of the side income that mattered—it was that it existed at all.

Plus, over time, those earnings don't stay small. That's because of a reverse take on the famous Latte Factor, coined by money guru David Bach. He argues that by spending money on a latte and other incidental expenses every day, you're costing yourself millions in the long run in lost compound savings. Using similar logic, earning a small amount every week or every month allows side-giggers to build financial security over time. Consider earning $200 a month through your side-gig. That's $2,400 a year. If you invest that $2,400 in an index fund that pays out 6 percent over the long haul, you have almost $40,000 after ten years. After thirty, you have over $200,000. Not a bad way to supplement a retirement fund.

To make sure we get the most out of those side-gig dollars earned, it can't just languish in a PayPal account—the mistake I made after running my Etsy account for a year. I had over $1,000 in the account, where it earned zero interest. Instead of splurging on new clothes or all the lattes I could possibly consume, I moved it to my savings account, where it at least earned a positive return while I pondered just what to do with the cash.

If these financial management details start to give you a headache, remember the bigger picture: If your full-time job is a bond, steadily paying a relatively modest rate, then your side-gig is your stock: It could take off at any moment, and make you rich, or at least financially secure, in the process.

TOP TAKEAWAYS

* The uncertainty of our economy necessitates finding new ways of earning income outside of full-time jobs.

* Some start-up costs are necessary, but there are ways to minimize them.

* Getting finances in order before launching a side-gig, including paying off debt and building up savings, can help increase the chances of success.

* Even small amounts of monthly earnings can add up to significant income over time, funding retirement or shorter-term dreams.

* The new identity that a side-gig creates can be just as powerful and important as the cash proceeds.

CHAPTER

4

Finding Friends

FROM THE OUTSIDE, ERICA SARA'S LIFE LOOKS LIKE THE PLOT OF A
Reese Witherspoon romantic comedy, but one that revolves around
the pursuit of business success instead of a man. She writes a blog,
where she posts favorite quotes. Recent samples: "The more you love
your decisions, the less you need others to love them." "Never get so
busy making a living that you forget to make a life." (She also writes
about adventures in cheese-making, decorating her own apartment
for the first time, and running races.) In addition, she maintains an
active Twitter account, where she sends encouraging notes to other
runners about their races. ("Congrats on the tri!") All of this outreach
is in support of her own jewelry-design business, Erica Sara Designs,
where she creates custom engraved jewelry.

A few years back, in her mid-twenties, Erica worked long hours as
a Coach merchandiser in New York City, helping to select handbags,
analyze sales, and track trends for the luxury brand. But even then,
she knew she had bigger dreams of launching her own business one
day. "I wanted to be able to be my own business. I was tired of working
twelve hours a day and not being gratified," she says.

While working full time as a Coach consultant, she started designing and selling her own jewelry. Friends offered to hold trunk shows

and helped her spread the word. "It was more of a hobby than a business before I realized that I wanted to make it a full-time business," she says. So she built her website and focused on defining her brand.

Since she's also a marathoner, Erica decided to focus on what she calls "race bling," which celebrates athletic accomplishment with inspirational mantras. "My jewelry is very tied to who I am," she says, adding, "I do any kind of mantra for people who want to send a message to themselves or out to the world about what they represent." She's created necklaces for people fighting cancer, losing weight, and celebrating anniversaries or relationships. More recently, she's also expanded into jewelry for mothers, featuring children's initials, names, and even footprints.

When it came time to launch her line, Erica leveraged the contacts she had already built up through her blog. "I realized that we're really lucky to live in this world today with Facebook, Twitter, blogging, and websites—there's this whole network of people that you can connect with, so aside from the people I knew in my own life, I started connecting with people online that I thought would find my line appealing." As a result, she says, "By the time I was ready to launch full time, I had people ready to buy on the first day." Despite the hefty start-up costs for engraving tools and gemstones, her company became profitable in less than two years. She attributes that success largely to the connections she made through social media.

In addition to her blog, she maintains Facebook, Twitter, Pinterest, and Instagram accounts, where she frequently posts about new designs, custom orders, and races. "It's really where I generate most of my business," she says of her various social media accounts. That closeness with her customers is also what she enjoys most about having her own business. "It's very personal and everything is custom. I know my customers and I know when their races are. I have customers email me because someone's mom is going through chemo and they want a necklace for chemo. That is what I love about what I do," she says.

Erica's blog has also helped her connect with a *Fitness* magazine editor, which led to her designs being featured in the magazine and another uptick in sales. She was featured in a *New York Times* story on the rise of running skirts, which ran alongside a photo of her jogging in a blue skirt through Central Park, her long brown ponytail swinging behind her. By finding her niche in the running world, building friendships, and leveraging them through social media, Erica turned her idea into a thriving jewelry business.

Across the country in Maryville, Missouri, and in a totally different field—wireless communications—Steve Lemler made a similar discovery about the power of social media. As the chief financial officer for a small wireless company that provides service to rural areas in the northwest part of his state, he became an expert in the quirky field of wireless company finances. In addition to standard financial statements, budgets, and internal controls, wireless companies in underserved areas must also file special paperwork to receive funds from the Universal Service Fund, which is designed to offset some of their costs. "Those filings are complicated," explains Steve, who's in his mid-forties. After he learned how to file them for his own company, he realized he could offer a similar service to other small wireless companies.

Through a previous job, he knew the founder of a start-up wireless company in Kansas. "All of his employees were brand new, and he didn't know how to do the Federal Communications Commission (FCC) filings, or the ins and outs of specific accounting for cellular companies, so he asked me to help him out and train his employees," says Steve. He showed the new chief financial officer how to account for various forms of customer revenue, as well as handle the FCC filings, which allowed the company to qualify for the Universal Service Fund. Steve, an accounting major in college, now spends about ten hours a week helping with this other company's filings. The work doesn't conflict with his full-time job, which he does between eight and five each weekday, because the start-up serves a different area. "We don't compete against each other—if we did, I wouldn't even think about doing it," he says. His boss, who's also a friend of the other company's founder, supports his outside work and even approves the occasional daytime conference call with the other company. The bigger potential conflict is with Steve's seven-year-old daughter, who maintains a vigorous athletic schedule, and expects her dad to cheer her on at softball games. "As she gets older, it's becoming more difficult," says Steve, but he still manages to squeeze in time for the extra work at night or on the weekends.

The added financial security that comes from his outside work lets him put money into his daughter's 529 account for college, as well as a Roth IRA for his own retirement. He saves at least 50 percent of the extra income for those kinds of long-term goals, and puts the rest into family treats (the most recent was a trip to Mexico).

Like Erica, he attributes his ability to earn a side income to his networks and online connections: He meets other managers of rural wireless companies at his industry's annual conference, hosted by the Rural Cellular Association. "We're all competing against AT&T, Verizon, Sprint, and T-Mobile, so all the small carriers work together," he explains.

That's allowed him to offer his financial services to other companies serving rural areas, including one in Arizona. "There's been a couple that I've helped get up and going," he says. "Whenever I meet companies at various conventions, I ask if they need any help. I want to help them out, and I'm also doing it because it pays me," he says.

He's also picked up work through LinkedIn. After the founder of the Kansas company left him a positive recommendation on the social networking site, a few clients contacted him and he helped them set up their filings. "It provided some brief extra income," he says—a source he knows he can continue to tap into whenever he wants, thanks to those connections.

STARTING FROM SCRATCH

Sometimes, side-giggers start their own online communities—and end up earning a living from them. Maria Sokurashvili discovered an utter lack of community for fellow new moms in the Washington, D.C., area when her son was born in 2000. She quickly set up a mailing list to help organize get-togethers. "Word-of-mouth grew, and people started signing up, and membership started to grow—first to hundreds, then thousands," says Maria, now in her early forties.

That's when she and her husband, Jeff Steele, a technology consultant, decided to launch a website, dcurbanmom.com. She knew moms wanted more information on everything from deciding whether to work or stay home to staying fit. Together, Maria and Jeff created over a dozen topic-based forums, and quickly added more, such as relationship and pregnancy sections, as interest grew.

As an addict to the site myself (I visit several times a day), I can attest to the need for it. When my daughter got her first 102-degree fever and the doctor hadn't yet returned my call, I asked for advice and received half a dozen responses within the hour. (Most of them encouraged me to give her infant Tylenol.) When my eight-month-old daughter still wouldn't sleep through the night, the anonymous ladies on the site gave me encouragement and told me that period would pass quickly and I would even look back on it fondly. (It did and I do.) The biggest value for me isn't in finding answers to those technical questions, but in being able to virtually meet up with a group of my peers who are struggling with the same issues as I am, to complain, find camaraderie, or just wallow in the fact that I'm not alone. New moms often feel lonely, and Maria found a way to connect us. And in doing so, she created a job for herself.

While they were growing the site, Maria also worked thirty hours a week as an information technology specialist for a small company. While Maria and Jeff hadn't originally planned to make money off dcurbanmom.com, they slowly added Google Ads, which covered the cost of hosting the site and their Internet connection. Soon, revenue from those ads started growing, and in 2011, just over ten years after first launching the site, the income was high enough to allow Maria to leave her information technology job for good. "Now, I can devote all my time to developing the site," she says.

She plans to improve and update the layout and work directly with advertisers to create more customized, and more lucrative, ads. Companies often contact Maria and Jeff about placing custom ads, but they currently have no method to do so, so instead they refer these advertisers to Google Ads, which means giving up potential revenue. "My first task is to develop a system that will allow us to work with advertisers directly," says Maria. Her new schedule means she has more time at home with her two kids, too—flexibility that wouldn't have happened had she not turned her new moms' network into a successful side-gig.

Emily Miethner, founder of NY Creative Interns, found similar success after she launched her company designed to help young creatives in New York connect with each other and with more experienced professionals. Six months after college graduation in 2010, Emily watched as her friends grew frustrated with the job market. "They were very talented but felt like they were going to have to settle for jobs they hated," she says. So she created a new group that connects successful creative professionals with up-and-coming recent grads. Her concept, which started with a blog and networking events, turned into a business when she and her cofounder, Reb Carlson, realized they could start charging for the events and picking up sponsors.

When Emily first started NY Creative Interns, she launched a simple Wordpress blog and created an account on Meetup.com, which described the group's goals of networking and navigating the job market together. "We used tags like networking, design, social media, internships, photographer," she says. Within a few weeks, fifty people had signed up, a fact Emily credits to the millions of people who go to Meetup.com to search for groups of like-minded people to join.

As the Meetup membership grew, Emily and her new partner, Marny Smith, worked on putting more content up on their blog. They had friends share recent job experiences and also interviewed people from well-known companies, including LinkedIn, AOL, foursquare, and Daily Candy, who then often shared the posts with their own social media followers. As the company started hosting more events, Emily always made sure to make it easy for the speakers, who were often from those same well-known companies, to share the event information online. "We always send out an email template for people, preformatted Tweets, and information for posting on Facebook—we make it easy for them," she says.

Facebook, Twitter, and Meetup are the primary ways people find out about events, Emily says, along with simple web searches. When people run a web search for terms such as "creative entry-level" or "creative internship," NY Creative Interns often comes up on top.

The blog now gets about 30,000 page views a month and the weekly newsletter reaches around 4,000 subscribers. Because so many volunteers are eager to work with the company (partly because it helps them make connections and find out about new job opportunities), Emily can outsource much of the work: A volunteer runs the blog and manages the guest bloggers who contribute to the site. Emily, who works full time as a community manager for a world records website, RecordSetter.com, spends weekends and evenings on NY Creative Interns.

Erica, Steve, Maria, and Emily each leveraged their knowledge and familiarity with their communities, whether it was fellow joggers, wireless communication workers, new moms, or newly minted creative people, to launch successful businesses. The fact that they were part of those close-knit communities is what first inspired their business concepts—Erica saw a need for race bling; Steve for financial expertise; Maria for better communication among local new moms; Emily for networking opportunities—and then their relationships helped them connect with their target markets. The ease of online networking, through blogging, Facebook, LinkedIn, and other social networking sites, generated more customers and steadily growing networks for all four side-giggers—and it can work for you, too.

Making Friends

To tap into your own networks to help build your side-gig, ask yourself these questions:

► **How can your current connections help you?** Do you have friends with "useful" connections? Are you part of professional organizations through work? Does your college or university have an active alumni association? Going to happy hours or connecting online can make it easier to find a mentor in your field or to find people who can offer referrals or help with promotion once your product or service is ready. If you're active on Facebook and Twitter, then you already have a built-in network—let them know what you're doing by linking, with a photo, to your product or service. In addition to receiving a boost from the congratulatory notes and "likes" that will inevitably follow, even if just from family members, your friends might offer other connections or suggestions that can help. (One of my writer friends caught a typo in my Etsy descriptions after I posted a link on Facebook.)

▶ **Would any of your current friends make good partners-in-crime?** Some people do better working in pairs or even threesomes; doing so allows you to double or triple your contacts, resources, and earning power. In her memoir *Falling for Me*, writer Anna David writes about why she decided to launch a book-editing company with a friend, another writer. "I've always done it a bit haphazardly, spontaneously deciding on my fee and trying to help in the best way I can. But if we band together, we decide, we can make it official: have set prices, a specific way of editing, and possibly even share clients," she writes.

▶ **How can you ramp up your social media presence?** To get word out about a specific product or service, you can create a dedicated Facebook page, which can feature photos, updates, and comments from customers. If you work in a visual field, consider building an Instagram account. If many of your potential customers are tech-savvy and permanently online, then building a Twitter following might be for you. For professional services, LinkedIn can work best. (Specific tips for building your social media presence in a way that will lead to sales are discussed in Chapter 5.)

▶ **What types of people or groups do you want to be more connected to?** If you work in a tech-heavy field, look for local tech happy hours or online groups. If you want to groom pets on the weekend, check out local dog parks and other gathering places. Browse Meetup.com for lists of local groups or run a web search on the terms that interest you, even if they seem unrelated, such as "gardening" and "urban patios." You might find that your niche already exists and has a dedicated following. While on some level these people are your competition, they will also become your support network. The leaders of your tribe might have written niche e-books on the subject or regularly give workshops on it; they might blog about their adventures or share them on Twitter. They will have valuable advice and contacts that they may even be willing to share with you.

► **How can you "stalk your tribe"?** Before making personal connections, research the networks you want to join by learning about them from their online trails. Facebook and Twitter accounts are prime starting points. When I wanted to learn more about online marketing, I used Twitter to follow the Rich Happy & Hot LIVE conference for women entrepreneurs run by marketing genius Marie Forleo. Not only did I pick up useful tips for free, such as focusing on one goal at a time, but I also started following dozens of other successful entrepreneurs on Twitter, which further widened my circle of online connections.

► **How do you like to connect?** Some people flock to happy hours like they're giving out free margaritas (sometimes they are); other people would rather send emails from their couch while wearing pajamas. If you prefer your conversations face to face, then happy hours and networking groups are probably for you; otherwise, social media is your savior.

► **If you could create any group, what would it be?** The answer to this question could even turn into a side-gig itself, as it did for Maria Sokurashvili and Emily Miethner.

JOINING THE CROWD

If your own niche isn't yet apparent, or even if it is but you want some extra support, then you can find help in the rich online community aimed specifically at people trying to get a side-gig off the ground. While many of these bloggers assume that the ultimate goal is full-time entrepreneurship, they have a lot of useful advice for anyone trying to turn a profit through their skills or passions.

Megan Moynihan Callaway was working for a big public relations firm in San Francisco when she started dreaming of a more mobile lifestyle. "It's all part of a plan that my husband and I have, so we can have professional careers that we enjoy, while being able to live wherever we want," she says. Since they love to ski, they want to live in Jackson Hole, Wyoming, in the winters and in New York for the rest of the year. Her husband, Ralph Callaway, recently left the website salesforce.com to start his own related consulting business. He loves the freedom that self-employment gave him, and his experience made Megan want to do the same.

As she continued working for her firm, Megan started quietly collecting her own clients, whom she met through friends. At the same time, she read up on how to run a small business on sites like Chris Guillebeau's blog (chrisguillebeau.com), which gives tips on earning money outside a full-time job, as well as LearnVest.com, which often showcases lessons from women entrepreneurs. She also relied on Google to bring her to the best sources for her most pressing questions. "I Google all the time—the top ten questions to ask to get feedback from a client, or questions to ask a prospective client, to understand their goals and what they'll use public relations for," she says. The Internet, and the blogs and websites she finds there, have become her new colleagues and mentors.

James Mundia, an information technology coordinator for a small association, similarly found inspiration to launch his own soccer coaching business after reading Ramit Sethi's blog, IWillTeachYoutobeRich.com, and taking his related course, Earn1K, on building a freelance business. James, who lives in Arlington, Virginia, and is in his late twenties, started offering private soccer training for young players near his home. His first summer session, which was promoted through a LivingSocial deal, was packed with fifty kids.

After meeting with two local community college officials to discuss using the college fields for winter training sessions, he got a call from them, asking if he'd like to interview to be head coach for the men's soccer team. The college offered him the position, which James calls his dream job—and now that's his second side-gig. It also lets him hire more people to help run the youth training sessions when they conflict with the college team's commitments.

The extra income lets him pay down his credit card debt and save money for traveling. The online support and advice he got from Ramit's blog and course helped him change the way he thought about earning money, and they also taught him how to ramp up sales. "I now feel like I could move to any city and have the ability to do freelance work that could help me pay my bills or just have extra money on the side," he says.

One of the earliest promoters of the side-gig concept, Pamela Slim (who refers to it as a "side-hustle"), also talks about finding ways to earn extra income through her website (escapefromcubiclenation. com). Pamela, author of *Escape from Cubicle Nation*, explains, "The concept became very clear to me as I was teaching people in corporate jobs who want to leave to start a business. Most people in that situation have significant financial obligations, and can't just quit their jobs. So I found the side-hustle to be a very wise strategy in order to mitigate risk." (She first heard the term "side-hustle" from a friend's teenage daughter who used it to explain why she does nails in dorm rooms to help pay for college.)

Like Chris Guillebeau and Ramit Sethi, Pamela inspires her readers to take action. "People spend far too long in planning mode. They have a hard time knowing how to put out a test of something to see if it works," she says. Her website, book, online courses, and personalized coaching encourage people to take that step. "You want to get [your idea] out to the market as soon as you can," she says.

There are dozens of other experts with useful blogs and websites, and more are launching all the time, including Entreprenette.com, CreateHype.com, The Young Entrepreneur Council (yec.org), Tara-

Gentile.com (from Chapter 1), and JonathanFields.com. When you're hunting for the website that will serve as your own personal cheering section, look for one that's tailored to your situation and goals, whether it's side-gigging in the corporate space, targeting female clients, or running an online empire.

FINDING MY TRIBE

As I struggled to get Palmer's Planners off the ground, I realized I needed a new group of friends. Not friends whom I could call after a bad day at work or to discuss my deepest concerns with—I already had those, and they were keepers—but a support group that I could go to with questions and encouragement whenever I got stuck in my creative business. I had so many questions: How could I market myself better? How quickly should I grow? Should I invest in paid advertising? By stumbling onto various blogs and books throughout the years, I had a vague sense that these people—people who were a few steps ahead of me in running their businesses, with lots of energy and answers to share—were out there; I just had to find them.

I started my search the traditional way, with Google. I typed in "creative entrepreneur." After scrolling for a page or two, I found a website that really spoke to me: Blacksburg Belle, written by April Bowles Olin, a former therapist and now full-time creative entrepreneur who makes her living through her creative pursuits, including coaching others. She looked to be about my age, and writes in a friendly, accessible way about topics I care about: the biggest mistakes creative entrepreneurs make, how creative entrepreneurs spend their days, and how to better manage one's time. Bingo!

Her site also pointed me toward another woman who would soon become an online mentor, Mayi Carles. Mayi creates gorgeous notepads and other crafty, organizational products that she sells through her own site as well as Etsy. She also blogs and makes videos about the life of a creative entrepreneur, and she soon became another rich source of free tips for me.

Passively reading their sites, though, wasn't enough. I wanted to become part of their communities. Both read and respond to comments left on their blog posts, maintain lively Twitter conversations, and feature business partners and acquaintances on their blog. I felt like the new girl, waiting to be invited to the popular girls' lunch table.

With a few proactive moves, I didn't have to wait for long. First, I signed up for both of their email newsletters, which kept me abreast of their new discussion topics, posts, and products. When Mayi released a free weekly planning guide, I snagged that, and I also picked up April's free goal-planning worksheet. I tweeted at each of them, praising the usefulness of their products. I left comments on each of their blogs, often answering questions that they posed in their posts, such as how to best manage energy ebbs and flows during the day. They each responded with thanks and comments; I already felt like I was getting closer to their inner circle.

One day, a month or two into becoming fans of their sites, I noticed April was releasing a new product that sounded perfect for me. It was a digital guide for creative types on how to market—my exact area of weakness. For a tax-deductible $22, it was mine.

I printed it out and spent the weekend pouring over it, scribbling notes to myself. She suggested getting word out about a new business by writing guest posts for other popular bloggers; that's how she ramped up the audience for her own site. She also said it was essential to define, to yourself and others, exactly what motivated you to launch your business. I started taking notes: "I want right-brained people to enjoy managing their money as much as they love creating art, or baking a cake. I want to break the intimidating world of personal finance into bite-size pieces that melt in your mouth. I want financial empowerment to feel good." A bit over the top, yes, but a version of that statement did eventually make it onto my Etsy shop page.

April warned against promoting a shop that wasn't yet fully stocked—if someone sees a storefront with just a product or two, they might just move on. While I didn't want to move too fast, I made a note to myself to further diversify and stock my store full of useful money-planning products as soon as I could. I also learned by studying how she marketed her own guide: One reason I bought it immediately was that she made it sound like she was exactly the expert that I needed—she loved marketing, she said, and she thought she could teach me to love it, too. I wondered if I could apply that line of thinking to personal finance: I love personal finance, and I want to help other people love it, too.

After devouring her guide, I tweeted at April about how much I enjoyed it, and she tweeted right back at me. It was almost like we were regular friends—almost. What we really are is virtual colleagues. When you're running a side-gig, you're typically working by yourself, rather than out of an office. That means instead of calling the corporate help desk when you run into trouble, or asking your cubicle mate for a brief tutorial on Excel spreadsheets, you're on your own. Until you find your new tribe, that is. This new group of people helps you become successful by sharing expertise, offering support and encouragement, and simply leading by example. As Ben Casnocha and Reid Hoffman write in *The Start-Up of You*, "The fastest way to change yourself is to hang out with people who are already the way you want to be."

Later, I talked to April about this kind of networking, and asked if she's ever turned off by people who are clearly trying to befriend her for their own benefit. If they leave comments solely to promote their own work, her answer is yes. She explains, "I think it's obvious when somebody's doing that as opposed to genuinely adding to the conversation or getting to know you, or asking questions for a good reason, rather than just promoting themselves. The people who are just leaving short comments with a link to something, you can tell they're just trying to promote themselves, and I won't have a good feeling when they contact me." Most people, though, are genuinely interested in contributing to the conversation, she says.

Now, when I'm struggling with a slow sales month, or receive a few rejections from bloggers who I was hoping would feature my planners, I visit Mayi or April's website, and remember that I'm not alone. Since I work in a traditional nine-to-five environment by day, I need to go elsewhere to feel connected to the more entrepreneurial side of me—the side that wants to create and sell planners. There are hundreds, perhaps thousands of people out there, just like me, trying to figure out how to earn a decent income by selling creative products. And sometimes, just knowing that is enough to keep me going.

I also discovered a more specific type of support, including feedback and suggestions for my Etsy shop, on Etsy itself. In the Etsy forums, shop owners ask each other questions and give advice. At first, I was scared to join the conversation, for fear that the more advanced Etsy sellers would laugh at my amateur questions. But I soon found that they were all just like me, eager to trade ideas and help each other. Even shop critiques contained gentle, helpful suggestions, such as "make your second photo lighter" or "lower your prices."

I learned that I should start using TweetDeck, which would let me organize my Twitter followers and also post to Twitter and Facebook at the same time. One shop owner wrote about the benefits of changing the name of her shop to something that inspired her more and better described her products. (My own shop name was boring, based on my first and middle initials and last name, since I had created it back when I was just an Etsy shopper, not a seller.) I also discovered that when mailing out the spiral-bound versions of my planners, I needed to pay more attention to packaging. Customers apparently appreciate small freebies and pretty tissue paper, so I ordered Palmer's Planners' bookmarks to include in each order.

As a result of one forum post, I created a discount code for my shop, so I could give it to customers as a way of encouraging them to spread the word to their friends. Another vigorous discussion shed light on whether or not to provide free products to reviewers who ask for them— the consensus was no, because it was a waste of resources. I also learned that I needed to focus more on the photos and images in my shop—they shouldn't just showcase my product, but evoke a lifestyle. As a result, I set up my spiral-bound money planner on our wooden dining table next to a turquoise mug, waited until the sun came through the window in early afternoon, and snapped one of my favorite shots.

For those selling through sites other than Etsy, an equivalent online forum most likely exists in a different form, depending on how and where you are selling or what type of industry you're in. Yahoo Groups, web forums, and even Facebook pages are prime spots to find those connections. Friends who are also working on their own side-gigs, even if they're in completely different fields, can become mentors and supporters—another reason to share your work on Facebook. After I posted a link to my planners, an old friend from middle school messaged me to say she had an Etsy shop, too. We traded tips on getting the word out and taking better photos. After getting to know the woman I hired to illustrate my planners, Lisa Nelson, I suggested that she pitch her stationery products to Paper Source. She got in touch with the company over Twitter and sent in samples. When I read a *New York Times* article about a new trend in high-priced "gender-reveal" cakes at baby showers, which tell guests whether the baby is a boy or a girl based on the pink or blue of the inner cake, I immediately emailed the story to Chris Furin. You never know where your next best idea will come from.

With my new support group behind me, I was ready to do more serious promotion and branding for myself and my shop. Those tasks, though essential, don't come naturally to me. I'd rather interview someone else about their work than talk up my own. But as uncomfortable as it made me, I had to get over that fear of seeming self-centered if I wanted to take my side-gig to the next level. Because promoting yourself, it turns out, is an essential part of creating the economy of you.

TOP TAKEAWAYS

* Social media often connects side-giggers to their communities, support systems, and first customers.

* Finding an online community or blog that's a source of encouragement, particularly one tailored to your own niche, can offer invaluable support and assistance.

* Web searches, Meetup.com, Facebook, and Twitter are among the tools that can lead you to your tribe.

CHAPTER
5

Putting It out There

ONE FRIGID JANUARY EVENING IN 2012, KATY GATHRIGHT WALKED with her friend Imran Khoja on the sidewalk along the main road that runs through the New England campus of Williams College, where they were both seniors. As they walked toward Katy's dorm, shivering as the wind whipped around their necks, Imran started telling Katy about a new campus competition that he wanted to join. Students could submit their business proposals to a committee, which would then pick a winner to receive $15,000 in seed funding, along with office space and other support. The only problem was that the competition required a second teammate, and Imran wasn't sure who to ask.

"I could do it if you wanted me to, as long as I don't have to do anything major," Katy told him.

"You're a genius!" Imran shouted. Even though Katy had thought he was hinting for her to offer her help, the thought hadn't yet crossed his mind. But now that he considered it, Katy was perfect: She already knew about his business idea, he trusted her, and they spent a lot of time together anyway. For the rest of the night, as Katy played beer

pong with a friend, Imran sent her a series of text messages full of reasons why she should join his team for the competition.

Together, they submitted a business proposal for what they call
Designed Good, a flash sales site in the tradition of Gilt or Zulily, but
with a twist: All featured products would not only be beautiful, but
they'd also be sustainably made. "The big idea was incorporating ethics and design, and doing it on a flash sales website," says Katy. A few
months later, while fleshing out the idea between class assignments
and senior year festivities, they won the competition, and made plans
to set up shop in Williamstown, Massachusetts, for the summer.

Katy, Imran, and a third Williams alum quickly launched the website, which allowed people to start signing up. Then, they started
reaching out to brands that they thought might want to partner with
them. They negotiated deals to sell the products at a big discount for a
limited time to their members; the site would earn money by charging
a small markup on those low prices. The first few products they
planned to feature included a refillable water bottle that filtered water
on the go, a company that upcycles old T-shirts into other products,
like blankets and underwear, and bamboo shirts. (Upcycling refers to
the process of turning old, discarded products into new and useful
ones.)

Because Katy had worked as managing editor of the college paper,
she created the company's blog. She posted about sustainability, what
it was like to launch the start-up, and products that caught her eye.
"We didn't plan it, but this whole aspect of storytelling behind the
products has been huge. It differentiates us in the marketplace. I want
our site to be a place you can hang out, read cool stories, and feel like
you can visit every day," she says.

In fact, her blog and related social media accounts, including
Twitter, Facebook, LinkedIn, and Pinterest, are the main reason that
500 people signed up to join Designed Good within weeks of launch.
"We're building community through content, so people don't just see
the products but they're also interested in reading stories," she says.
She might profile a twenty-five-year-old New York City dweller who
started an urban garden, or how other twenty-somethings are
launching socially conscious businesses, or send a tweet to a popular

fashion blogger who might be interested in exchanging guest posts. (I discovered Designed Good after Katy posted a link on the LinkedIn page of my high school, where she is an alum as well.) She's also guest-posted on other websites to help spread the word. And when new members sign up, they're immediately encouraged to invite friends, using financial incentives: Sign up ten friends, and you can pick up a twenty-dollar credit toward your next purchase. (They later changed their referral system so anyone who gets two friends to join receives free shipping.)

Blogging has helped Katy and Imran define their brand: "We want our website to embody a person—an older brother or older sister who has awesome ideas and awesome stuff that you aspire to have, and they have a bit of a socially conscious edge," she adds. They also get valuable feedback; when a few blog posts on the upcycled underwear got a lot of buzz, they decided to feature that product in an upcoming sale. On Pinterest, Katy takes note of which products get the most repins and comments as part of her market research into which types of products will resonate most with members.

Just like Erica Sara and her race bling jewelry in the previous chapter, Katy thinks blogging helps potential customers feel that they know and trust the brand. And that helps her take her business to the very important next stage: making sales. In fact, Designed Good's social media presence is one reason why she thinks the company got such a high purchase rate on the first test run of the refillable water bottle: Out of 100 people notified about the sale, 17 people made the purchase—an exceptionally high rate for an online campaign.

Katy learned a central lesson about getting word about a new product or service: Earning trust, explaining why you exist, and letting people get to know you—all parts of building a brand—are essential to making people feel comfortable enough to buy from you. And putting the word out there often means stepping outside your comfort zone.

ALMOST FAMOUS

Celebrities have learned the importance of branding as well. Super-models, who can expect their career highs before age thirty, often try to meld their reputations into something broader than just beauty so they can parlay their fame into a second career. Heidi Klum turned herself into a fashion icon, clothing designer, and host of *Project Runway*. Cindy Crawford launched skin care and home furnishings lines. Karolina Kurkova works as a host for high-end celebrity events while she considers her next step, possibly a line of baby products. Even young models know they have to build their brands early; twenty-something supermodel Coca Rocha gives her peers lessons on making the most of social media. (Coca herself has around 500,000 Twitter followers and maintains an active, and popular, Tumblr account.)

The supermodel lesson applies to the rest of us, too: If our full-time jobs eventually disappear, then our personal brands can make it easier to find new employment, and quickly. Those brands are as valuable to us as a medical license is to a doctor. It's what allows us to build our own following of customers, clients, and fans, even as we move from one venture to another. (Being distinguishable from our coworkers through a personal brand—if we're known for our expertise on, say, marketing through social media—can also make our bosses more likely to keep us around. We're not quite as replaceable by the latest, more affordable recent graduate.)

It's those brands that enable us to opt out of the bidding wars that take place on popular freelancing sites, where graphic designers living in India can underbid designers in urban American cities every time, because people pay more for something they know.

Among the many side-giggers with strong personal brands that I came across, April Bowles Olin, whom we met in the previous chapter, seems to exemplify "strong branding" best. Through her blog, video posts, and product descriptions, April, who has the dark hair and enthusiastic demeanor of Rachael Ray, comes across as someone you want to have on your side: She's friendly, creative, professional, and clearly loves her role as a promoter of creative businesses—and she knows exactly what she's talking about.

While it looks like she's just being herself, April consciously built her brand over time. She started in the online world over five years ago with a wedding planning blog that focused on do-it-yourself strategies, from bridal headbands to create-your-own invitations. But after she got married, she wasn't as interested in wedding cakes or bridal veils anymore.

Eventually, she settled on a new brand for herself: Blacksburg Belle. She had already been selling her jewelry on Etsy and fielding questions from people on how to do something similar, so she decided to start writing about how to build a successful creative business. All of her blogging was on the side: Her full-time job was as a therapist, working with at-risk adolescents in New York. "I was getting so emotionally involved with families and wanted some kind of creative outlet at home," she says. She started offering group coaching lessons through the site, and soon quit her therapy work to focus full time on her creative business. She now earns about four times her former salary as a therapist.

April's secret success formula is obvious to anyone who takes a quick glance at her site. Her unique brand, and what she has to offer you, the visitor, is immediately obvious: She can help you grow your creative business. She can teach you how to excel in marketing, even if you think you hate it.

When she started blogging at her new site, BlacksburgBelle.com, she made sure her posts offered useful information to readers—specific tips on how to grow a business. At first, she spent more time writing for other people's blogs than her own; guest-posting was the main way she got word out about her new site. As a result of email pitches she sent to other popular bloggers, she was featured on BlogcastFM. com and wrote a guest post on DesignSponge.com, which led to 300 new newsletter subscribers in one day. "I was working my butt off to get featured any place that I could," she says. Her efforts paid off: Soon she started getting 800 page views a day, and today over 5,000 people have subscribed to her email newsletter.

Along the way, April continued to build a sense of trust and loyalty with her readers by sharing a mix of personal and professional stories; she emphasizes the importance of sharing your "why," or what drives you to create your business. "People want to buy from a person, especially if it's handmade stuff or you're providing one-on-one services," she says. The better they understand and trust you, the more likely they are to ultimately make a purchase. She finds that most of her customers who buy group coaching lessons are long-time subscribers to her email newsletter. "I already have relationships with them built up over time by providing content, so they know I'm the real deal and not going to scam them," she says. In her newsletters, she often shares personal stories, about a conversation she had with her husband, or why she used to hate trying new foods. To get the right tone, she says she asks herself, "How would I say it to a friend?"

Now, thanks to her brand, April doesn't have to spend her days pitching potential bloggers and clients. As a result, she recently shared with her newsletter readers, "I have people contacting me daily who've found me via features, interviews, and guest posts." She doesn't have to look for them anymore, because they're finding her.

Melissa McCreery, cofounder of the career website The Daily Muse, used a similar strategy to take her site to the million-user mark within ten months of launching. Melissa and her two cofounders, Kathryn Minshew and Alex Cavoulacos, who all worked as consultants for McKinsey & Company right out of college, quickly realized that they had a lot to learn about the workplace. "We felt like we needed guidance and the right mentors. I did have a good mentor, who helped me with how I presented myself, how to manage people for the first time, and little things I did, like how raising my voice at the end of a sentence made me come across as more junior," she says. While she and her cofounders originally focused on young women, they soon discovered that many young men were just as interested in the career tips.

That's why she and her cofounders launched The Daily Muse, designed to help people in their early twenties. Melissa and her cofounders, now in their mid-twenties, launched the site in September 2011, with a carefully honed brand in mind.

They knew their target audience—ambitious professionals in

their twenties who are trying to get ahead—and they started connecting with them by writing quality articles filled with useful advice, from how to bring your lunch to work to how to avoid burnout. The articles were so good that *Forbes* and Huffington Post started syndicating some of their content, which brought them more readers. Arianna Huffington even wrote a piece for The Daily Muse to kick off a series called "Lessons to My Younger Self." (She wrote about how she wished she had gotten more sleep.)

The next step was engaging their readers so they kept coming back. Melissa and her team did that by soliciting guest articles from readers. "From there we built a community of writers who saw what we were about," she says. Those contributors, who ballooned to over 200, write about topics they themselves struggle with, such as how to make it as a freelancer, how to negotiate a salary, and how to navigate a career transition.

"That played a big role in building our organic audience," says Melissa. "They would come back, share their articles with their friends, and feel like they're part of our community and building it with us," she adds. The site also became packed with an array of diverse perspectives and fresh content. "We weren't just relying on a handful of staff writers, but people from all industries and all walks of life," says Melissa. The site's related Facebook, Twitter, and Pinterest accounts also helped attract more readers, especially for visual content such as how to pack a lunch salad inside a mason jar. (Put the dressing in first.)

About ten months after launch, The Daily Muse was garnering 300,000 unique visitors a month and growing about 30 percent a month. Melissa and her cofounders—who participated in the start-up incubator program Y Combinator, based in Mountain View, California—raised angel investor funding and are making plans to continue growing. (Angel investors give money to start-ups, often in exchange for some kind of ownership that will pay off if the start-up becomes successful.) Revenue comes primarily from the company profiles and related job listings hosted on the site; organizations ranging from Groupon to Teach for America pay a monthly subscription fee to participate. Says Melissa, "We want to be the go-to resource for professionals navigating their careers. When they're thinking of making a move, or need advice, or get promoted and want to negotiate, we want to be the resource people know they can go to." That's the definition of the Daily Muse brand.

BRANDING 101

We all already have brands, even if we don't know it yet. If someone wants to find out about you because they're considering hiring you for a job, then they're probably going to run a web search on your name first. Whatever comes up—their impressions of you from your public presence—is your personal brand, for better or worse. The key is to make sure that the web search reveals exactly what you want it to. (Your brand, of course, extends into the offline world as well. References, coworkers, acquaintances—whatever they say about you also contributes to your brand.)

The easiest way to do that is by creating a website or blog that explains who you are and what you offer the world. Even a simple site with just a bio, photo, and links to past work can work. When you write the bio, describe yourself the way you want the world to see you: If you want to be a writer and speaker, then describe yourself as one, even if you've only done a couple of gigs so far. To some degree, simply calling yourself a speaker, or a coach, makes you one, because potential customers can now see you in that light and consider working with you. Then, you can link to that page through your existing social media accounts, such as Facebook, and when anyone mentions you online, they can link to this page, as well. With enough incoming links, this main page will be the one that pops up first after web searches. (If you have a common name, or share a name with someone who is more famous, then you'll have to work a little harder to get your web page noticed.)

This website should tell people who you are, and what you can do for them. Perhaps it's dishing out career advice, or telling them how they can pay off debt. Maybe you will be their gardening guru, or go-to vegan cupcake source. Whatever your specialty, this site should clearly answer the question: What makes you different?

While you don't have to spend much money on it, the site should look clean, professional, and appealing. For less than $100, you can hire a freelance graphic designer to create a custom header. To find one, ask your favorite bloggers for recommendations, or pose the question to Twitter or Facebook friends. You should also consider buying the URL for your name or business so you don't have the cumbersome "wordpress.com" or "blogspot.com" words in your online address. As for web hosting, you can stick with a free service such as wordpress.com and redirect the page to your URL, or you can pay a monthly fee to upgrade to a hosting service.

From there, building a brand requires a similar etiquette dance to dating: Just as on a first date, constant self-promotion is a major turn-off. Interaction, and asking about other people, is a plus. Dale Carnegie, the self-improvement guru, had it right when he urged people to act interested in others, to never offer public criticism, and to smile. I'm always surprised when someone uploads a photo of themselves scowling as their Facebook or Twitter image. It doesn't make me want to follow them. An updated version of Carnegie's classic book, *How to Win Friends & Influence People,* spells out how his advice applies to social media. If you want to criticize someone, he says, do so offline, in private. Public Twitter or Facebook spats are usually embarrassing for everyone involved. Some bloggers use it as a strategy for stirring up controversy, but it can easily backfire. Responding to other people's comments online should more closely resemble cocktail party chatter than a bar fight. People who are only talking to themselves over Twitter start to look a bit like wallflowers, or, even worse, like narcissists. As for your photo, Carnegie's book points to research that shows that people who smile in their Facebook photos tend to have more friends.

While you're ramping up your audience, an email newsletter can help, too. Sites such as MailChimp.com or ConstantContact.com make it easy to create good-looking newsletters for little or no money. Once you have people's email addresses, then you have more control over when you reach them. If you're launching a new product or service, you can let your email newsletter subscribers know first, and even offer them a discount or free bonus for their loyalty. As April Bowles Olin puts it, "It's super important to have a way of reaching people that's all yours." She also needed her newsletter as a backup when her Twitter account went down during one of her program launches.

When I was first launching what would become my popular USNews.com blog, Alpha Consumer, in 2007, I learned quickly that people responded most enthusiastically when I shared my own personal stories with money: why I found buying a car so stressful, how my parents taught me about money, and my irksome interactions with the customer service arm of my health insurance company. Those posts garnered the most comments, and my readership really exploded when I started hosting contests and trading guest posts with popular money bloggers. Other reporters and television producers looking for a money expert to feature started stumbling onto my site through web searches and asking me to appear in their articles or on their shows, which led to more links and a higher profile for my blog (and for me).

As April found, linking to other sites and having them link back to you can quickly spread word about your blog, and as long as your content entices, those readers will often stick around. (This is also where having influential friends comes in handy. If you already know a few popular bloggers from networking events, Twitter, or leaving comments on their blog, then they're far more likely to take you up on an offer for a guest post.)

Your site also has to make it clear what makes you stand out from the thousands of other blogs out there—do you offer entrepreneurial tips for creative types, like April? Or help empower consumers, like my Alpha Consumer blog? Or help connect people to socially conscious, beautiful products, like Katy and Imran's Designed Good site?

Because our media world is so fractured—newspaper readerships are dropping, and people depend on multiple smaller sites instead of one catchall news source—building up a fan base through a website or blog can give you as much power, or more, to ultimately sell your products and services than even a positive review in a big newspaper or magazine.

Making people care about you, and convincing them that you can help them, is the key to finding lasting (and paying) customers.

If you're really struggling with marketing yourself and, like me, feel like it's your weak spot, then there is another option: You can hire professional help. You can pay someone to Tweet for you, set up a marketing campaign, or even send pitches. The problem is that professional publicity help can cost more than a five-star trip to Italy. One author told me that she spent about $7,000 a month for nine months to promote her book, for a total of $63,000. That's clearly not even an option for most of us, and even if it were, spending that much doesn't guarantee media hits, or sales. But the even more important reason to learn how to do the marketing yourself is that it's an invaluable skill, one that can continue to help you in both your full-time job and future side-careers. (And if you do hire professionals, they will likely want to make use of any personal connections you have developed on your own anyway.)

Still, it can make sense to invest in a few upgrades: a professional website design, an e-book on social media marketing, or a group coaching course like the kind April offers. Part of being a good marketer means getting help when you really need it.

Branding Checklist: Grade Your Progress

Answering the questions below will help you sharpen your focus and take your branding/marketing activities to a higher level:

► Who is your ideal client or customer? (Be as specific as possible, including a description of their gender, age, hobbies, and location.)

► What's the best way to reach that target audience? Where do they spend time online? What websites or blogs are popular among that demographic?

- How do you currently reach out to potential clients or customers?

- Who are your current customers and how are they finding you?

- What could you do to reach more people?

- If you run a web search for your name, what turns up? What do you wish turned up?

- What do your social media accounts say about you?

- Have you spread the word about what you're offering by telling other people in your field, who offer similar but distinct products or services? How could you help each other?

- How are you creating your own community of like-minded people—people who can become customers? Do you offer a blog, newsletter, or other type of free content to attract potential fans?

- What is your biggest weakness when it comes to marketing and how could you get help with it?

THE ART OF THE PITCH

For certain, highly specific enterprises—if you're targeting, say, pregnant women who are vegans, or lawyers who also run marathons, where there might only be a handful in your area—then targeted pitching, combined with word-of-mouth marketing, is often the way to go. It's the main strategy Peter Davis, now in his early twenties, chose to spread word about his new community-building website, CommonPlace (ourcommonplace.com).

Peter, a recent college graduate who sounds and acts more like a college professor, launched his site while he was still in school. In a scene reminiscent of *The Social Network*, he and his roommate were sitting at lunch talking about applying to summer internships at the end of their freshman year at Harvard. They started talking about how useful it would be if there was one centralized website that listed everything that was available in each city. "That idea expanded past college kids looking for internships. We thought, 'Why don't local places have a place where you can share and connect?'" Peter recalls.

That conversation led to CommonPlace, a website that offers towns a centralized website for community members to talk to each other, buy and sell things, and announce events. It's that middle piece—the buying and selling—that Peter and his cofounders plan to turn into a moneymaking enterprise, by charging a small fee for such exchanges. (The site, including Peter's modest salary and those of his cofounders and employees, is currently funded by angel investors.)

Instead of waiting for towns to hear about the site and request a customized version, Peter and his team actively reach out to towns they consider good matches for part of the early launch. "We just pick towns and go in. . . . We don't want to wait for the mayor to call us," says Peter. Once they choose a town to target, he sends a handful of community organizers who spend six weeks handing out flyers, working with community groups to spread the word, and signing up local teens, dubbed "junior civic heroes," to interview leaders in town and post those interviews to the site. The organizers also start up a Facebook page and Twitter site to help promote the new website, and contact local media for potential coverage. As the company reaches more towns, Peter plans on doing more outreach over the phone and web, to make it possible to ramp up more quickly.

While Peter and his team currently pick towns based on proximity or other connections they have—one of the first towns was Peter's own hometown, Falls Church, Virginia—they also sometimes respond to requests they receive on their website. The strategy has already shown results: CommonPlace is currently in a dozen towns and has over 10,000 users, and the company is constantly reaching out to new towns. Peter has big plans: "We want to be in all 18,000 towns in America."

Lucinda Lyon-Vaiden, who practices traditional Chinese acupuncture and therapeutic massage in the Dupont Circle neighborhood of Washington, D.C., also adopted a highly specific, targeted strategy when she first started taking on clients. Instead of advertising to the general public, she told her friends and coworkers about her new practice. For the first ten years of her business, she worked as a meeting planner during the day and met patients between 4:30 p.m. and 7:30 p.m.—and found all of her clients through word of mouth.

That's exactly how she wanted it. "I didn't want to do a big splash in the Yellow Pages because when you get referrals, it's self-selecting. It's not someone coming in off the streets who wants to negotiate the price or time. Especially if you're doing massage, you could get a lot of creeps." Instead of creeps, she got "friends and colleagues, and then their friends, their sweethearts, their wives, bosses, and families," she says.

Lucinda's ultra-targeted marketing strategy got her exactly the type of clients she wanted: They tend to have an interest in holistic health, and often share useful articles and research that they've read with Lucinda, too. "People tell me about everything from herbs, medicine, research studies, and food, so it's a two-way street. They keep me up on stuff," she says.

Lucinda explains most of this to me as I lie face down on her massage table; I've been seeing her for several years to help counteract lower back pain. Her office (she rents space with a group of other health practitioners) is filled with anatomical diagrams, health textbooks, and the soothing CD of nature-inspired music. As with most of her clients, a coworker introduced me to her, and her focused, minimalist style appealed to me right away.

As soprano Renée Fleming writes in her memoir, *The Inner Voice*, reaching out to the potential clients or customers (or in her case, venues) that you want is the best way to take control of your career. Her manager, she says, "stressed batting instead of fielding—actually proactively deciding what I wanted to do, rather than just considering the offers as they came in." If you want to make things happen, you have to create those opportunities for yourself. Writing a pitch forces you to ask yourself what types of opportunities you really want, who your ideal audience or customer is, and what exactly you have to offer that holds value for others.

Perfecting the Pitch

A good pitch is personalized, clearly describes what you have to offer, and explains what the recipient will get out of accepting it. If you're pitching your graphic design skills to a popular blog, then you're more likely to get a response if you make it clear you are a fan of the blog and know her writing well, and that you could design a header or widget that would help the blogger appeal to her audience. Pitches often get deleted right away if they aren't addressed to the recipient by name (a simple "hello" doesn't work), if they contain a lot of text-heavy paragraphs without proper grammar (a red flag for spam or just poor writing), or if they seem overly self-promotional. Luckily, there's a whole world of free resources to help you with self-promotional language because so many people struggle with it. DuctTapeMarketing.com, copyblogger.com, MarieForleo.com, and ChrisBrogan.com are a few of the top resources.

My dad, an environmental film producer and professor, often tells his students, who need to learn how to pitch their film ideas to potential producers and funders, that the most important factor in an effective pitch is enthusiasm. "Pitching is never going to be easy, and if you don't believe in your idea, then trying to get someone else to believe in it is virtually impossible," he says. Telling the story of how you came up with the idea can often help convey that enthusiasm.

As an example, here's one of my successful pitches to a personal finance blog:

Hi Phil,

How are you? Last time we spoke it was about your book project, how is that coming?

I thought I would let you know about my latest personal finance project just in case you have any interest in blogging about it or otherwise mentioning it any way. . . . I just launched Palmer's Planners, a line of financially themed planners aimed at helping people navigate major goals and life events. What makes them different—and I thought you would like this part—is that they take a creative and visual approach to managing money, in order to appeal to right-brainers (like myself). The planners include The 2012 Money Planner, the Debt-Free Planner, the Baby Planner, and the Money Planner, which is designed as a workbook for my book, *Generation Earn*. They're all on Etsy, http://www.etsy.com/shop/kspalmer.

The planners are all based on my reporting and interviews with people on what really helps them reach money goals, which usually revolves around figuring out just what those goals are, breaking them into smaller steps, and getting organized enough to stay focused on them.

If you have any interest in mentioning any of the planners in any way, I would be most appreciative, and could send tips, checklists, excerpts, cover art, or anything else that would be helpful. I would of course be happy to send over digital copies so you can see the planners for yourself!

Thanks for considering it!

Kim

As you can see, I personalized it, explained my bigger goal (helping people with their money), and then briefly described what the planners are. The blog ended up featuring my Money Planner and led to at least a dozen sales. (The Handbook at the back of this book includes a pitching worksheet, which you can also download at economyofyou.com.)

PLANNER PROMOTION

As I had discovered from my own initial lack of sales, publicity matters—a lot. No one can buy from you if they don't know about you. And for the first month of my own Etsy shop's existence, barely anyone knew about it, which is why I made just one sale. Checking my stats and seeing no new orders was a little depressing. It felt as if I'd thrown a birthday party and no one showed up.

Getting word out isn't easy, and it's where a lot of side-giggers get stuck. Sure, some people seemed to magically acquire a massive customer base, including Amy Stringer-Mowat, who stumbled into coverage in *Real Simple* and other women's magazines, and Chris Furin, who had a built-in fan base from his father's deli. But most people have an experience more similar to mine—they have to work for their customers, or they don't have any at all.

As I started pitching to bloggers, I focused on reaching out to personal finance and parenting sites, offering guest posts or giveaways of my planners. I sent emails to a dozen popular baby blogs, explaining my baby planner and how it would help soon-to-be moms navigate those overwhelming nine months. Over time, I learned to become more efficient. The popular design blog that I'd previously had no contact with? Probably not going to respond to my email. The mommy blogger who lives in my neighborhood? Definitely a better shot. And as for the personal finance blogger that I had previously featured in my own blog, that was almost a sure thing.

Still, sometimes I didn't hear back, and on a couple occasions, I got a flat-out rejection or simple note saying that they don't do guest posts or that my baby planner looks too similar to a product they sold themselves. I quickly deleted the offending emails, tried to forget they ever existed, and moved on to the next pitch. A few kind bloggers said they liked what I created, and offered to help me promote it. One popular mommy blogger linked to my Etsy shop on her Facebook page, which brought me a couple hundred views. A personal finance site reviewed my Money Planner and hosted a giveaway; another invited me to write a guest post. As word got out, a few bloggers wrote to me to ask if they could feature my planner and host a giveaway. Despite the Etsy forum warning about giving away too many freebies, I always said yes. Even bloggers who didn't feature my planners often wrote nice notes back, which helped me build a broader network.

I quickly realized that I had the most success with editors of personal finance websites that I had already worked with. After explaining my new project to them in a way that got at my goal of giving people creative tools to get on top of their money, they often wrote back and said they would be happy to feature my planners. My biggest traffic days—and sales days—came after the women's finance site DailyWorth.com featured my planners and baby blog LilSugar.com highlighted my Baby Planner. Close behind were blog posts on TheCreativeMama.com, a blog for moms, and several personal finance sites. Because these websites had such large followings, they continued to direct traffic to my Etsy shop even months after the original feature. They also led to write-ups on smaller blogs and websites. I'd discovered the snowball effect of free advertising.

With the publicity came the orders. During my launch month, November 2011, I sold 33 planners, earning $438.40, and picking up over 3,400 page views on my Etsy shop. Almost all of my traffic came from the Facebook links and websites that had agreed to feature my planners. Those sales continued through December; by the end of the year I had sold 65 planners and earned $864.80. Some mornings, I woke up to three or four orders that had come in when I was sleeping.

Sales continued to pick up as I responded to customer feedback. I noticed that some customers were purchasing more than one planner at once, so I created "money planner kits," which offered discounts on multiple planners. My Complete Money Planner Kit, a package of three planners, became my top-selling item. The 2012 Money Planner came out of an idea from a customer and fellow Etsy seller, who told me that she wanted some kind of calendar that she could follow as the year progressed. I soon added more "money kits" to the mix, including the Homeowner's Complete Money Planner Kit and the New Parent's Complete Money Planner Kit. I also quickly realized that the digital PDF versions of my planners were far-outselling the spiral-bound, printed versions, so I stopped stocking those once my initial supply ran out. For customers looking for an easy reminder of their goals to post near their desks, I worked with my illustrator to create a simple one-page "money goals" planner that could be filled with specific goals, challenges, and action steps.

By the end of February, I had sold over $1,200 worth of planners. I noticed a direct correlation between the number of people viewing my shop and the amount I earned: My revenue always seemed to hover around 10 percent of the total number of page views. That meant the more publicity I did, the more I would make. Marketing is time-consuming, though, so while I tried to pitch a few websites or blogs each month, it was hard to keep up the intensity of launch month. As my marketing efforts simmered down, my sales stayed constant at around $200 a month.

As gratifying (and useful) as it was to earn that extra cash, it didn't even begin to get at the satisfaction that my Etsy shop gave me. Each sale affirmed my ability to create something of value, a skill I sometimes doubted that I had as freelancing rates plummeted during the recession and writing jobs dried up. I had a new identity; I created and sold money planners. I began daydreaming about ways I could expand and new products I could design. Perhaps I could offer coaching sessions in tandem with my planners; I could create a career transitions planner, a "working mom" planner, and maybe even an "eat better, spend less" planner. I wondered if one day I would open up a physical shop, with space for people to fill out their planners and brainstorm about their lives, next to a coffee bar and sign-up sheet for one-on-one coaching sessions. I created a new listing in my Etsy shop for a "personalized" version of my one-page money goals planner, which included talking with me about how to reach specific financial goals. After a few months, I sold my first personalized goals planner (for $60), and got to experience serving as a money coach—and I liked it.

While my Etsy shop grew, I also spent time marketing myself to potential speaking gig hosts. On my website, I added descriptions of financial workshops and talks that I give, such as "How to Be a Financial Rockstar," along with a photo of me speaking and a list of recent speaking events. After reading Robin Fisher Roffer's branding book,

Make a Name for Yourself, I more clearly defined my niche—navigating the financial milestones of adulthood—a theme I emphasized on my website. Whenever I spoke with other personal finance authors and speakers, I tried to mention my new focus on giving talks, and as a result, several of them passed on speaking requests to me. I also put the word out to magazine editors that I was looking for more free-lance assignments. As a result, more requests started coming in.

Soon, I was completely overwhelmed. Between spending time with my daughter, my job, running my household, and building my side-business, I felt like I was constantly sprinting when what I really wanted was to settle in at more of a marathon pace. (Nap time only lasts so long, and the laundry—not to mention my husband—also demanded attention.) I needed more time—for myself, for my family, for my work—and I needed to figure out how to get it.

TOP TAKEAWAYS

❋ Building a social media presence that reflects what you offer—and what you want to offer—is a key step toward finding paying customers.

❋ Mastering the art of pitching yourself and your product to potential clients and bloggers is essential to spreading word about your business and landing paying gigs.

❋ For highly targeted businesses, personal connections and referrals can be even more important than a social media presence.

CHAPTER
6

Time Is Money

IT'S A GORGEOUS, EARLY SUMMER, 75-DEGREE DAY, BUT INSTEAD OF using my lunch break to get some fresh air, I'm headed to the bottom level of a hot, smelly parking garage in downtown Washington, D.C. Jessi Baden-Campbell, a meeting planner for a consulting firm by day, is using her lunch break to rehearse for her role in an upcoming opera at the Capital Fringe Festival, a local celebration of the performing arts. Jessi, a professional opera singer, invited me to watch, and learn how she combines a full-time job with an almost-full-time singing career, all while raising two children under the age of five.

As we make our way down the staircase to the very bottom of the garage, Jessi explains that she has to go all the way down to minimize her chances of disturbing people in the lobby. Her voice is so powerful that it carries three flights up, even through concrete. Since she practices three times a week, parking garage attendants have come to expect her lunchtime concerts.

She sets out her binder with song notes, iPhone, and water on a nearby Honda Civic, and presses a few keys on her piano app to get the right notes. After warming up her lips with a rolling "brrrrrrr" sound, she belts out Wagner. The acoustics are incredible: Her voice bounces off the garage walls and resounds throughout the garage. If I close my eyes, I can almost pretend I'm at the Vienna Opera house, despite the occasional roach and the extremely unpleasant smell of car exhaust.

As Jessi transitions from her Wagner warmup to the English lyrics she will perform at the Fringe, she uses her hands to gesture, and mutters mental notes to herself. "So don't breathe there," she says, when she runs out of air at the end of a line. After taking in the full force of her powerful voice, I wander up the garage ramps, to find out just what the parking attendants can hear from the upper levels. Her voice carries around the turns of the garage, until eventually, near the top, she sounds like an ocean siren from Greek mythology, luring sailors closer to rocks until they crash. Indeed, office workers who catch a drift of her voice often wander down to see what's going on.

While Jessi, who recently turned forty, would prefer to focus exclusively on her opera career, she discovered that the lifestyle frequently required dropping everything for weeks of rehearsals and performances, often in a new city—not an easy thing for a mom to do. She also found that building a dependable income as an opera singer was close to impossible, especially after the recession hit and dried up funding for the arts. Before she had children, she was willing to take those risks, and accepted a series of freelance performances. She moved to Anchorage, Alaska, for four months to perform at the Anchorage Opera, and also performed at the Des Moines Metro Opera and Nevada Opera in Reno. She earned rave reviews in national publications; the *Washington Post* called her "vocally powerful and physically imposing."

Once her daughter was born, her priorities switched. "You can't expect your child to sacrifice meals and their own comfort, so I got a full-time job," she says. She relegated her singing career to the side while working forty hours a week as a meeting planner. She picked up steady work at a local church, which requires a Thursday night rehearsal and Sunday morning performance; she earns about $10,000 a year for that. She also sings for a local synagogue during the high holidays, which involves months of preparation and four solid days of singing. For that, she earns another $5,000 a year. She also supplements with the occasional wedding or corporate performance, which can pay up to $500 per appearance. Other workshops or performances, for which Jessi usually uses up vacation days, can pay $800 for three to four days of work, not including rehearsal time. To find potential opportunities, she stays in touch with friends in the performing arts and occasionally posts about her availability on wedding chat boards.

Jessi and her husband use her singing income to pay for household expenses, such as new windows for their house in Falls Church, Virginia, and savings for their children's future college tuition as well as their own retirement. Since they live in an expensive city with two children, that income stream feels essential to their family's financial security.

After forty minutes of working out her vocal cords, it's time for Jessi to grab lunch from a nearby food truck to eat back at her desk before her hour-long break is up. As we walk back up the three flights of stairs, Jessi mentions that she'll head to rehearsal for the Capital Fringe opera right after work; it's from 6 to 9 p.m. every night for the next month. "How do you handle that, especially with being a mom?" I ask her. That time slot seems like prime parenting hours, typically filled with dinner, bath time, and books.

She admits it's hard. "Sometimes when I get home, I cry," she says. It's a lot of pressure, and she often feels guilty about not spending more time with her son and daughter. She invited her mother-in-law to live with the family, so she can fill in when Jessi has an unexpected performance or late-night rehearsal. Her commitments to the church choir mean that much of her weekend is taken up, and she doesn't have many vacation days left since she dedicates most of them to performances or workshops. On one recent Sunday, she woke up to sing at a 7 a.m. church service, stayed for the 10:30 service, and then drove an hour away to perform at a wedding.

But as she explains why she does it, her tone changes from one of frustration to gratitude. "I don't want to become a bitter person who had to give up her art," she says. "I'm committed to myself as an artist and I'm also committed to my family—in order to spend time with them, and to provide for them financially, while also feeding myself in terms of my own passions and my own movement forward as an artist, I have to make the time," she continues. Plus, she knows her kids understand, and support her. She pulls out her iPhone to show me a video of her four-year-old daughter proclaiming that she wants to be a singer just like mommy when she grows up. Jessi is clearly imparting invaluable lessons to her children, even when she's at a rehearsal.

LEVERAGING THE DAY JOB

The secret to excelling in both a full-time job and a side-gig is often to find a way to combine them, in a completely aboveboard, ethical way. That means your boss knows what you're doing and is happy about it, because it brings your employer some kind of related glory or benefit. (Exactly how much you share with your boss depends largely on the office culture in which you work, which varies widely from company to company. You'll want to get a keen sense of how side-gigs are viewed before talking up your own—and the examples that follow showcase a wide range of possibilities.)

That's not to suggest building a side-gig, even one related to a main gig, is easy. Almost all the side-giggers I interviewed struggled with finding enough time to meet their multiple responsibilities. Just as jobs have become less stable, they've also become more demanding. A 2011 survey by the Society for Human Resource Management found that instead of adding more positions when they needed to get more work done, employers instead ask their current employees to do more. Almost one in four hourly employees said they worked longer hours compared to earlier in the year. Indeed, many side-giggers work demanding jobs, putting in fifty hours or even more each week. Yet they still find ways to excel in the side-pursuit, usually because they are able to use their full-time job as a lever to boost it.

For Jennifer Teates, a law firm manager in Annapolis, that means turning her experience working on collections and bankruptcy issues into a writing career. "We have lots of people calling in and they don't know basic information—what seems to me like common sense," says

Jennifer, such as how much personal information to share with creditors who ask where you work or where you bank.

Jennifer, who's in her mid-thirties, realized she could help people by sharing information about navigating debt settlement and bankruptcy, so she started contributing articles to Yahoo! Finance and then contacted her local editors at Examiner.com about writing a personal finance column for them. After an application process, they hired her, and she soon started writing for Motley Fool as well. Since her day job provides story ideas and expertise, it feeds right into her freelance work.

To get her writing done, she wakes up around 5:30 a.m., two hours before her toddler son gets up. That way, she fits in a couple hours of writing each day before heading to the office (or telecommuting from home). That doesn't leave a lot of time for sleep—around six to seven hours—but Jennifer says that's all she needs. She insists she doesn't have a Type-A personality, and fits in plenty of relaxation time in the evenings, starting with family dinner time.

The schedule requires plenty of planning, but Jennifer says she's living exactly the life she wants. In addition to enjoying her writing, it gives her financial security: "If something happened, like my law firm decided to shut down one day, I can fall back on freelance writing. For now, I just sock away the money I bring in," she says. She has plans to grow her writing career further, with a comedic financial planning book in the works.

One thing she doesn't plan on doing is leaving her law firm, even if her writing career takes off. "A lot of my ideas come straight from my office, so it would be really silly to drop my source of information," she says.

That was also the case for Jeffrey Nash, inventor of a new kind of baby walker that he calls "the Juppy." In the summer of 2011, just as my own baby was mastering the ability to walk and run, I got an email pitch from Jeffrey, who said he had figured out the best way to impart this skill to young children. He described the Juppy as "an alternative to dangerous wheeled baby walkers," and as a paranoid new parent, my ears perked up. Anything that claimed to add to the safety of my child captured my attention (and often my money).

When I called Jeffrey to talk about writing a potential story on his product, I discovered that he had invented it while employed full time elsewhere: a suit store. Jeffrey, now in his late fifties, had spent much of his working life as a salesman, working the floors of a Las Vegas Men's Wearhouse. Then, one day, he found himself facing a major pay cut and more competition from younger, cheaper salesmen. As much as he loved his job and prided himself on his ability to make his customers happy, he knew it wasn't going to last for much longer.

One day, while watching a mother help her toddler walk, he had a big idea: What if he created a new kind of baby walker that allowed parents to give their toddlers assistance without bending over and straining their backs? Through his retail contacts, he figured out how to establish a patent and mass-produce the prototype. When mothers with babies shopped for tuxedos at the Men's Wearhouse, Jeffrey pulled out his prototype and asked them to try it, then made adjustments based on their feedback. Any time customers mentioned they were pediatricians or doctors, he solicited their endorsements. Customers who worked in marketing connected him to local news producers, who featured them on their programs. His job, while completely unrelated to his side-business, enabled him to make the connections he needed to get the word out about his product. "I showed everybody to see what they thought. It helped me tremendously," he says. He says his supervisors didn't mind because he was working and selling suits at the same time.

During a three-week vacation from Men's Wearhouse, Jeffrey marketed the Juppy at baby product conferences and reached out to online retailers and baby stores. "Whenever I could corner you, I did," he says of his salesmanship. During that three-week period, he sold $12,000 worth of walkers, and that was just the beginning. The Juppy has since been profiled on the *Today Show* and Jeffrey expected to bring in $250,000 in annual sales soon after launching, and double the following year. He eventually quit his Men's Wearhouse job and now works full time as the chief executive of his company, but not before benefitting immensely from the connections and customers at his previous employer. Says Jeffrey, "Had I not done this, I would have ended up homeless at some point in the next ten years." Instead, he went from earning $65,000 with shrinking benefits at Men's Wearhouse to running a company that's growing fast.

Ebony Utley, an associate professor at California State University Long Beach in the communication studies department, similarly uses her position as a means of advancing her outside pursuits. In 2009, when the California State University faculty union agreed to a furlough, she found herself with extra time on her hands, and a need to earn some cash. The move meant a 10 percent pay cut for all faculty, including Ebony, along with two furlough days per month. "I said, 'I need to make it up in another way,'" Ebony recalls. That's when she launched her second career, which involves speaking, writing, and managing her website, TheUtleyExperience.com. "Teaching is awesome, but I want to have a broader audience than just the students in my classrooms," she says.

Ebony used her academic expertise in pop culture, race, and romantic relationships to become an outspoken expert on those topics. After emailing her friends and colleagues in academia to pitch her services, she started traveling to different universities to guest lecture on the role of religion in rap music, sexism in hip-hop, and how pop culture portrays black women versus the reality of their lives. In one lively talk at the University of Dayton, she explored how Amber Rose, former girlfriend of Kanye West and current girlfriend of Wiz Khalifa, used her dating life to get ahead professionally as a singer and model. She went on to argue that the hip-hop generation is continuing the legacy of the civil rights generation by celebrating African American culture and uniting different ethnic and racial groups.

Around the same time, Ebony started blogging for popular websites, including *Ms. Magazine*, Religion Dispatches, and Truthdig.com, on topics from Maria Shriver's divorce to interracial dating. She also wrote her first book, *Rap and Religion: Understanding the Gangsta's God*. In her author photo, she's dressed like a rapper, with a white fur wrap, dark lipstick, and huge gold earrings. If you look quickly, you might think you're looking at Rihanna.

To balance her new career with her professorial work, Ebony adopted a strict writing schedule: She gets to work first thing in the morning. "I get out of bed, have tea, and start writing," she says. On days she's not teaching, her friends know not to call her until noon. "I learned to fiercely protect my writing time," she says. She sets her timer for 120 minutes and makes herself write for at least that long, but often finds herself going for another few hours. Ebony keeps a log in an Excel spreadsheet of all the time she spends writing, so she can see her progress and also gauge how long it takes her to complete certain projects, such as writing an article or a blog post. "That way I know that if I need twenty-four hours for something, I can plan to do it over spring break, or in the summer. That log changed my life," she says.

Ebony also works with what she calls an "accountability partner," or a friend who works in her field who helps keep her on track, and vice versa. They talk about their projects, deadlines, and progress, and often swap drafts of work. "Writing is a lonely life, but having a peer give feedback makes my work stronger," she says. (She also squeezes in some downtime every day when she's home to watch her favorite show, *The Young and the Restless*.)

Just like Jennifer Teates and Jeffrey Nash, Ebony's secret is that she uses her full-time job to advance her second career: "I started teaching more classes that fed directly into my public intellectual work. I designed the first hip-hop class for my department, and a pop culture class, so everything I had to learn about to teach those classes were also things I was blogging and speaking about. My students came alive more in the classroom when they saw what I do, too," she says. If her worlds didn't dovetail, "there's no way" she could handle four classes a semester in addition to her speaking and writing work, she says.

Combining a side-gig with full-time work doesn't always go so smoothly. For Melissa Van Orman, it took a bit more wrangling, and eventually, a major life change. At first, she lived the life of a typical side-gigger: She woke up early, often before the sun came up, to get to her health consulting job by 8 a.m. or earlier. She had to bill at least forty hours a week, which meant nonstop days packed with meetings and phone calls. Then, by 5 p.m. she would rush out the door to make it to the yoga studio where she taught packed evening flow classes to the after-work crowd. She usually left the studio after 9 p.m., headed to her nearby home, and collapsed in exhaustion. "Physically, emotionally, energy-wise—I couldn't sustain that," says Melissa, who's in her late thirties.

At the urging of her husband, she eventually left her consulting job to become a different kind of side-gigger: one who juggles a full-time yoga teaching schedule of both classes and private clients with part-time teaching work on nutrition and health at George Washington University. "I took a $50,000 pay cut, and it was right when the economy was imploding, but it was the best decision I ever made," says Melissa. Her new schedule meant that she could fit in her yoga classes and client meetings, as well as preparation, throughout the day, instead of cramming everything into the evenings. She also recently picked up an additional freelance job as a health writer for the Centers for Disease Control, where she previously worked, which has helped make up for that initial loss of income. She noticed that when she stopped working her office job, her spending dropped significantly: She makes her own lunches, buys fewer clothes and shoes, and spends less on convenience items such as taxis and takeout. "Not working in a conventional way has really freed us up," she says.

The reason she says she can now handle so many different jobs at once is largely because they all fit together and build on each other: Her teaching experience in the yoga studio makes her a stronger teacher in the classroom, and her yoga studies contribute to her nutritional expertise. (In addition to her advanced yoga training, Melissa also holds a master's degree in health communication.) Before, a lot of tension came from the fact that she felt that her yoga teaching conflicted with her consulting work: "I was seeing my colleagues publish papers and speak at conferences, and I realized that during the twenty hours a week I was teaching yoga, they're doing that—I felt like I was only giving half to each of those things."

Now, Melissa's flexible schedule means that she not only gets everything done, but she also ends each day feeling relaxed and fulfilled. She typically works seven days a week, and often starts the day at 5 a.m., so she can make it to a 6 a.m. private client yoga session. She might have another client later in the morning, and go home for a leisurely lunch on her own. In the early afternoon, she'll often head over to the university to teach her nutrition class to undergraduates, or fit in her freelance writing work from home. (She can walk to both the yoga studio and university from her apartment.) Then, her evening yoga classes begin around 6 p.m. and go until 9 p.m. Her husband, who works for the government, often leaves the office to take her evening classes, so they can spend that time together. "In some ways, it sounds exhausting to have a seven-day-a-week schedule, but I also have three hours in the afternoon where I can take my dog to the woods and walk him, or grocery shop. I work when other people are off, so it makes it easy. Or I'll take a twenty-minute nap in the afternoon if I get up early for a client," she says. What she doesn't have, she says, is time every night to watch television or cook dinner, but that's a trade-off she's willing to make.

OPPOSITES ATTRACT

When side-gigs don't feed directly off full-time jobs, there are often other ways to turn each identity into an asset that boosts the other. Twenty-something Nicholas Ignacio attributes his success with his lawn care business to one factor: that he's also a full-time college student. That fact, he says, is why clients hire him, trust him, and pay him more than minimum wage. Everyone wants to support local college students, he says.

As a criminal justice student at Marymount University in Arlington, Virginia, he joined up with a friend who suggested starting a power washing business. When they went to register at city hall, they needed a company name, and came up with "Strong Students Lawn Care," which ended up shaping their business. His clients come primarily through his Craigslist.com listings and word of mouth.

To keep up with demand—just a few months in, his company was already fully booked three to four days a week—Nicholas hires other trustworthy college students as employees and spends his time visiting client sites, providing estimates, and taking care of administrative work. He also reaches out to new clients, including banks, realtors, and commercial companies. Still, he says, "I have to make school a priority," which is why he schedules his lawn care work for the days he doesn't have classes. He's able to pay for his living expenses with that income. His work supports his college lifestyle, and it's that identity that allows him to land so many jobs.

Other side-gigs are so impressive—like Jessi's opera singing—that supervisors and coworkers are often happy to provide support by granting a more flexible schedule when necessary. They're proud of the side-pursuit, and perhaps appreciative for the additional glamour that it brings to the office. At the very least, they don't see the side-gig as something that takes away from the full-time job.

That's certainly the case for Alisha Williams, who competed in the U.S. Olympic 5,000-meter, 10,000-meter, and marathon running trials for the 2012 London Olympics. (You might have caught her blond ponytail racing around the track.) Alisha, who works full time as a certified public accountant for an energy company based out of the Denver area, says her coworkers and supervisors are always excited to hear about her races. Before her Olympic trials in Eugene, Oregon, her officemates threw her a party and decorated her desk with U.S.A. signs and streamers. While she didn't quite make it to London (she came in fifth place in her 10,000-meter race), they are still proud to have an (almost) Olympic-level athlete among them.

Through careful planning and Outlook calendar management, Alisha avoids conflicts with her day job, or giving her accounting work short shrift. It's not easy, given that most athletes competing at her level work only part-time jobs or dedicate all of their time to the sport.

Alisha joined an Olympic development program after college, while she was starting her accounting career, but she didn't see her times change much. "I thought of myself as just a jogger," she says. She continued to build her career, studying for the CPA exam, earning her license, and putting in sixty hours a week at the office. Her low point was in 2007, right after tax season ended, when she ran a 5K race in what was (for her) a record slow time. "My husband watched and he was like, 'Were you even trying?' At the time, it was hard to do the running thing and the full-time professional CPA thing. You want to do your best and give it 100 percent," she says.

That's when she decided to get serious. She tried for the 2008 Olympic trials but came up short, and later found out she had an iron deficiency. She joined up with a new coach and training team, The American Distance Project, a nonprofit dedicated to training U.S. distance runners. Her CPA job also became more predictable and stable, requiring closer to forty to fifty hours a week instead of sixty-plus. While she emphasizes that her top priority is her day job, she says her schedule lets her run in the morning. She typically wakes up between 5:30 and 6 a.m., drinks some tea and has a snack, then gets out for a run with her husband and dog. Four days a week, on what she calls her "easy days," that means running ten miles in the morning, along with drills. Then, she works for eight or nine hours, and runs again, three to five miles in the evening. On the other days, she does her more intense workouts, which might consist of warming up for three miles, then running an extensive series of 400-meter sprints, followed by a two-mile cool down. She runs another four miles in the evening and heads to the pool. She saves her long, eighteen-mile run for Sunday, and swims in the afternoon.

To keep herself going, Alisha eats plenty of fruits, vegetables, protein, and smoothies. She and her husband make smoothies with spinach, Greek yogurt, and protein powder after their morning runs. Some evenings after her evening runs, she eats an almond chocolate bar. Then she tries to get in bed by 9 p.m.

If her race schedule ever conflicts with work, she tries to work ahead as much as possible. "I don't have the luxury of waiting until the last minute," she says. She adds her running commitments to her office Outlook calendar so her colleagues know about her schedule in advance. (She uses vacation days for her races.)

Without her accounting job, Alisha could have experienced what many other Olympic-hopefuls experience after almost qualifying for the Games: crushing disappointment, and confusion over their next steps. Shortly after the 2012 Olympic trials, the *Washington Post* ran a story on how bereft many athletes can feel after almost making it. Only a small fraction of Olympic trial competitors became one of the 530 athletes to make to the Summer Games. The problem caught the attention of the U.S. Olympic Committee, which now offers athletes job placement help, career coach consulting, and resume advice.

Athletes like Alisha, who already have careers outside of athletics, don't need to depend on that kind of assistance. "If I had to rely on [income from running] that would be hard. I don't feel the added pressure that people who only run probably feel; the need to do well to pay the rent," she says. Still, some years her running earnings are significant enough to add to her financial security. Those earnings come mainly from sponsorships—Alisha is sponsored by Boulder Running Company, Adidas, and PowerBar—as well as race prize money. (After speaking with Alisha, I discovered other Olympians who share her approach, pursuing full-time careers alongside their Olympic ambitions, which gives them financial security during and after their training. Natalie Dell, a health care researcher at the Veterans Affairs Department, won a bronze team medal in rowing in London. Triathlete Gwen Jorgensen is also a tax accountant at Ernst & Young.)

Now, Alisha's already planning for the 2016 Summer Olympics in Rio de Janeiro, when she'll be thirty-four. After that, she plans to continue to balance her running career with her accounting work. "I don't ever want to stop being active, and running is my favorite activity," she says.

Corinne Delaney also found that even though her side-gig as a classical singer isn't directly related to her full-time job as a graphic designer and training analyst for a government contractor, her employers still see it as a major asset, and even occasionally use it to their advantage at company events. She highlights that she is a classically trained singer on her resume, and says that potential employers have asked her about it during job interviews. "[Classical singing] goes hand in hand with discipline, and shows I pay strict attention to detail," she says.

Earlier in her career, when Corinne, now in her mid-thirties, was interning at the American Trucking Association, her coworkers asked her to sing "Danny Boy" at the president's birthday party. Shortly afterwards, she was bombarded with performance requests from coworkers. Not only were her supervisors impressed with her talent, but the performance helped her pick up new clients for weekend singing gigs.

Today, as a full-time employee for CACI, a large government contractor whose acronym originally stood for California Analysis Center, Inc., she performs about once a month at weddings and community events. While Corinne says she performs for the "sheer joy" of it and is often happy to donate her talent for charity, her regular paid performances typically pull in several hundred dollars or more, depending on length and location. Her voice, strong and clear, transports the listener; her rendition of "Somewhere Over the Rainbow" sounds simultaneously modern and traditional. In addition to her performances, Corinne, who has been training as a vocalist since she was fourteen, gives lessons to a small handful of students and plans to soon release a recording. She's now using her skills gained from her full-time work as a graphic designer and training analyst to develop a website that will help take her singing career to its next level.

Stephanie Theodore's second career brings a similar kind of glamour to her day job, but in a totally unrelated field: art. By day, she serves as a department manager at a major financial firm in New York City. On the weekends, she runs her art gallery, THEODORE:Art, in Brooklyn. Stephanie, who's in her early fifties, often spends her evenings meeting people, helping the artists with their installations, and getting word out about upcoming exhibitions by emailing her newsletter list or writing press releases. Her day job requires about forty-five hours a week of her full attention, although she can often squeeze in emails or Tweets during slower moments.

Her bosses are well aware of her work in the art world, and they like to joke that her management job is her "side-gig." She gets great annual reviews and is recognized for being supremely organized and balanced. "I'm artsy for my day job and I'm pragmatic for the art world," says Stephanie, who holds a master's degree in art history.

She avoids potential conflicts by maintaining a strict schedule: She's in the office during the day, and then on the weekends wakes up early with her dog, around 5:30 a.m. They go for a walk together, and she does some shopping, and then she bikes to her gallery from her apartment in Queens. "I build in leisurely enjoyment to the whole process," she says. Her gallery is open to visitors on Friday through Sunday from 1 to 6 p.m. (She's there for the weekend hours.)

She also skips things she considers unnecessary. She doesn't get manicures or pedicures, she avoids television, and she doesn't spend much time getting her hair done. "My feet are not pretty, and I don't care—of you're looking at my toes, you're not looking at the art on the wall or listening to what I'm saying," she says.

"I've always had this dual life," says Stephanie, and she adds she wouldn't want it any other way. She gets her financial security from her office job, and her creative satisfaction from running her own business. In some ways, she's following the example of her father, who worked in advertising but would spend two-hour lunch breaks looking at art at the Museum of Modern Art. "We're all artists, and we all do what we want, but we have to be able to pay for it, too," she says.

COMBINING UNRELATED (AND POTENTIALLY CONFLICTING) CAREERS

When the two pursuits are completely unrelated and neither pursuit seems to add to the other, then getting both done can require a bit more creativity and strict adherence to legal and ethical guidelines. But even side-giggers playing a zero-sum game find ways to make it work.

Martin Cody, a vice president of sales for a medical software company who works from home and the founder of Cellar Angels, an online wine marketing company that contributes a portion of sales to customer-selected charities, operates with extreme efficiency. In fact, before he agreed to speak with me, he asked me to answer a series of questions about exactly what I planned to ask him and what I hoped to get out of the conversation. Every night, he writes down the five things that he must get done the next day. "Normally a to-do list might have thirty to forty items, but there should be five critical ones," he says. He makes a separate list of five for both his full-time job and his wine business, and he keeps a legal pad by his bed in case any ideas pop up during the night.

During the day, Martin, who lives in Chicago and is in his mid-forties, keeps two computers on his desk in his home office, one for each job, and he manages to respond to emails and take care of other tasks related to both businesses simultaneously, all day long. He also wakes up early, between 4:30 and 5 a.m., to get started on the day. He makes calls for his wine business after 5 p.m., when his sales job has wrapped up but the wineries in California that he works with are still open for business. He might work seventy hours a week or more between his two jobs, but he also makes time to walk by Lake Michigan, visit farmer's markets, and, of course, drink wine.

Martin's idea for the wine business came during the 2008 recession, around the time that Groupon launched. He wanted to figure out a way for wine stores to participate in the group coupon movement. "Unlike a lot of merchants, who can have a discount one day and not the next, a winery has one product a year, so they can't do that. They also get solicited by charities all the time," he says. Since his wife runs a wine store in Chicago, he already knew the industry well.

Cellar Angels offers weeklong discounts from small, California wineries to website members (out of view to the general public, so as not to hurt the value of the wine), and also allows customers to contribute a portion of those sales to specific charities. "It hit me like a flash: how do you honor charity requests, gain exposure for wine, and solve the consumer problem of access to wine from these small wineries?" That's how Cellar Angels was born, and it's quickly picked up steam, partnering with Leeza's Place, Leeza Gibbons's foundation that supports family caregivers, and Generation Rescue, Jenny McCarthy's autism organization.

Martin plans to continue growing it, alongside his medical sales work, but because the two are unrelated, he keeps them completely separate, just like his desk setup: two different computers, working side by side. In fact, his bosses at his medical sales company don't know about his wine work. "I haven't concealed anything, I'm just not actively promoting it," he explains. For now, that's the arrangement that seems to make the most sense, and so far, it's working.

Dana Lisa Young, a website content manager in Atlanta in her early forties, found herself in a similarly polarized situation, juggling a forty-hour-a-week office job with a growing wellness business, where she practices Reiki, reflexology, and life coaching. The two jobs are as different as wine and medical sales: Her content management work involves sitting at a desk, developing internal and external company websites, along with editing and posting content. Her wellness business consists of one-on-one client sessions and workshops where she helps promote healing and health. Since her wellness work is done mainly on the weekends or after work, when clients usually want to meet, it rarely conflicts with her content management work. Her employers are aware of her outside work, and when she worked a nine-to-five office job, they also knew that it was never scheduled during work hours, and that the work itself didn't create any conflicts of interest. When Dana worked for a professional services firm that had to abide by Securities and Exchange Commission (SEC) regulations, that distinction was especially important. She reported her business information to a database that was updated each year.

"The corporate environment and wellness business are worlds apart," says Dana. That dichotomy sometimes led to a bit of culture shock when she went straight from the office to see clients. In the early days of her business, she often worked nonstop for weeks at a time with no days off; like yoga teacher Melissa Van Orman, she found it exhausting. And like Melissa, she eventually decided to rearrange her schedule to fit in more downtime. She went from a full-time content management position to contract work, which allows her to work largely from home and for fewer hours each week. That gives her more time to grow her wellness business, as well as to attend school events and be with her children.

Dana still does much of her client work in the evenings and on the weekends, when her husband can be with their children, and she works during the day on her content management responsibilities. That leaves her with spots of free time to squeeze in laundry or to blog, Tweet, or write a Facebook post about her business. She puts all commitments on her Google Calendar, and schedules blocks of time for work and family. When her children go to bed, she often gets back on the computer to work. She also meditates before getting out of bed in the morning, to guarantee that she fits in some relaxation for herself every day.

Dana earns less now, but, like Melissa Van Orman, says that trade-off is worth the additional flexibility. "I really objected to the fact that in most of these jobs you're required to give 120 percent of your time, even if they say work–life balance is important. At some point I felt, 'This lifestyle isn't worth it to me,'" she says.

Some people allow that tension they feel between their full-time jobs and side-gigs to build until it explodes. When the now-famous novelist Jeffrey Eugenides worked as an executive secretary for a poetry organization at the beginning of his career, he secretly spent his time in the office writing his novel, *The Virgin Suicides*. *New York* magazine reports that he would type on office letterhead to try to escape notice. But it didn't work; his bosses noticed and he got fired. For side-giggers who like and depend on their full-time jobs, that's a disastrous outcome. It's also one that can be avoided, even when the two pursuits don't mix well, by finding ways to create time in non-work hours.

Traditionally, the thinking has been that if you're going to pursue a little something on the side, then at least have the good sense to keep quiet about it, as Martin Cody does. I even wrote about that school of thought in my first book, *Generation Earn*, and quoted career coach Pamela Skillings on the concept. She encourages people to keep their outside projects under wraps so no one suspects their true passions are located elsewhere. That strategy probably works best in the most traditional of office settings, where people still slowly climb the corporate ladder. In the 1960s drama *Mad Men*, partner Roger threatens to fire account manager Ken when he finds out he's been writing science fiction novels after hours. "Your attentions are divided," Roger warns him. "As an account man, you have a day job and a night job." A chastised Ken quickly agrees to stop writing. A small subset of people might find themselves in a similar predicament today. If that's the case, the side-gigger will have to make a tough decision, to give up the side-gig or find a more flexible job.

In most modern workplaces, though, this way of thinking feels as outdated as Don Draper himself. Many successful side-giggers find that their full-time workplaces fully embrace their side-pursuits and, in fact, see them as assets. That's a good thing, too, because Facebook,

Twitter, and the rest of the Internet make it virtually impossible to keep secrets anymore.

Minting Minutes

When you need to find ways to squeeze more hours into your week, you can cut out certain activities that previously took up a lot of time, wake up earlier or stay up later, or simply become more efficient so you can do more in less time. Side-giggers mentioned the dozen strategies below over and over again:

► **Wake up insanely early.** Setting an alarm for the crack of dawn clearly isn't for everybody, but it was by far the most commonly cited technique for getting more done. Nicole Crimaldi Emerick, the founder of Ms. Career Girl from Chapter 1, does it, along with The Accidental Creative's Todd Henry (Chapter 2), and writer Jennifer Teates. Khaled Hosseini, bestselling author of *The Kite Runner* and a doctor, has said he woke up at 4:45 a.m. to write his novel before heading to work at the hospital.

► **Make use of slivers of time.** Brief moments of downtime, while you're waiting for a bus or in line at the bank, can easily be wasted. But they can also be put toward a side-gig instead. Douglas Lee Miller, the social media consultant from Chapter 3, works on his mobile devices while commuting to his full-time job at DePaul University. Jessi Baden-Campbell uses her lunch break to sing in the parking garage. Stephanie Theodore responds to quick emails while at her financial firm. *Glee* actor and children's book author Chris Colfer told *Entertainment Weekly* that he wrote his fantasy novel, *The Land of Stories*, between shooting scenes while sitting in the makeup chair. Karen Thomson Walker wrote parts of her bestseller, *Age of Miracles*, on the subway as she headed to her job as a book editor.

► **Commit to doing less.** If you want to run a side-business, maybe your toes won't always be perfectly manicured. That's the trade-off Stephanie Theodore decided she could accept. Peter Davis, the founder of CommonPlace, decided he didn't necessarily need to make straight As if it meant getting his project off the ground. Melissa Van Orman says she's okay not cooking dinner in the evenings or meeting up with friends after hours; she'd rather have time to teach her yoga classes.

► **Sequence your work.** Maybe you don't have to work a forty-hour week all the time. Ebony Utley decided to take a year-long sabbatical from her teaching commitments at the first opportunity she had. That's what will allow her to start work on her next book, on infidelity in real life versus the way it is presented in pop culture, while continuing to promote her speaking career. Life coach Jenny Blake took a three-month sabbatical from Google when her book, *Life After College*, came out. Reiki practitioner Dana Lisa Young and yoga teacher Melissa Van Orman switched from full-time office jobs to contract work to make more time for their side-businesses. Morgan Hoth, the silk scarf creator, waited until she retired from her teaching job to ramp up her business.

► **Incorporate time with loved ones into work.** Runner and certificated public accountant Alisha Williams runs with her husband; Melissa Van Orman's husband attends her evening yoga class. Maria Sokurashvili, founder of DCUrbanMom.com, started the site with her husband, and it became their joint project; app developers Beena Katekar and Sudhansu Samal used the same approach.

► **Build relaxation into the routine.** For Dana Lisa Young, that means meditating before getting out of bed; for Ebony Utley, it's taking time to watch *The Young and the Restless*. Jennifer Teates puts her toddler in a jogging stroller and takes him for a spin around the neighborhood shortly after he wakes up. Stephanie Theodore rides her bike from her apartment in Queens to her art studio in Brooklyn on the weekends. Financial coach Glinda Bridgforth, who also works as a writer, speaker, and board member, spends time looking at the Detroit River every day, which she can see from her home office.

► **Focus on energy management over time management.** All hours are not created equal; you might be able to get more done at 10 a.m. than at 7 p.m., or vice versa. Dana Lisa Young is most productive on the computer in the after noons and evenings; for Jennifer Teates and Ebony Utley, morning is prime time. Planning work during those peak productive hours can lead to much greater output.

► **Cut back on television, Facebook, and other time drains.** To some people, a no-television rule sounds despotic; some of us need our *Real Housewives* episodes to unwind. But others, including Martin Cody, swear by this rule. Martin calculates that by skipping half an hour of television every night, he gains almost 200 hours of extra time a year.

► **Live by your calendar.** When you're juggling multiple jobs, they can all fit on a shared calendar, such as Google Calendar or Microsoft Outlook, to keep commitments from conflicting with each other. That's how Alisha Williams ensures important meetings don't land on race days, and how Martin Cody avoids scheduling wine meetings during sales calls. Career coach Ford R. Myers, who also consults and speaks, has used a week-at-a-glance calendar for twenty-five years, and fills every line with appointments, to-dos, and reminders related to his multiple ventures. He likes to see the entire week in front of him without needing to scroll around on a screen.

► **Ignore other people's priorities.** Your boss deserves your attention, but everyone else who asks for it might not. I started saving myself hours each week when I simply stopped answering my office phone when a number I didn't recognize popped up. It was almost always public relations professionals pitching products I was unlikely to cover.

► **Consolidate household management.** Ordering groceries and almost everything else online, hiring a professional cleaning service, and using websites like TaskRabbit.com to outsource tasks such as cleaning out a garage can save hours—hours that can then be dedicated to your side-pursuit. If you'd rather not spend the money to outsource those tasks (or can't afford the help), then you can focus on getting them done as efficiently as possible so at least part of your weekends can be devoted to your side-gig. Indeed, the American Time Use Survey published by the Bureau of Labor Statistics in June 2012 found that most people (57 percent) who hold more than one job spend time working on the weekends, compared to 33 percent of people who have just one job. That suggests side-giggers use Saturdays and Sundays to make progress on their side-pursuit.

► **Write every idea down.** Martin Cody keeps a pad of paper by his bed in case he has an idea in the middle of the night. I email myself about five notes a day related to Palmer's Planners or other projects; the ideas usually come to me when I'm jogging or driving, and emailing myself as soon as I can use my phone again is the quickest way to record them and make sure they're not forgotten. It also makes for an easy way to delve back into work the next time I'm at my computer.

THE POWER OF NO

After my first book came out, I worked hard to promote it, writing dozens of guest blog posts and appearing on as many television and radio shows that would have me, no matter how small the audience. This work could take up to ten hours (or more) each week, and of course it didn't come with a paycheck. But I was happy to do it, because I wanted to spread the word about my book.

Even after those initial months of post–book launch, I kept getting requests for guest blog posts, to appear as a guest on podcasts and online radio shows, and to speak to small groups. For a while, I kept saying yes; after all, if even just one person bought my book because of it, I felt satisfied. As a result, my typical work week, which already exemplified the harried juggle of a working mom rushing from preschool drop-off to work and then back for preschool pickup, became even more hectic. As soon as I put my daughter Kareena to bed, rushing through *Goodnight Moon* as quickly as possible, I'd race down to my basement office for a Skype interview with a blogger. Then, it was back upstairs to start preparing her lunch for the next day and making dinner. My husband, who was usually just arriving home from work, and I would quickly eat before collapsing in bed.

The last straw came when a local political group asked me to speak to them about getting their finances in order. Since that's one of my favorite topics, I happily said yes, even though it would be an unpaid gig. The host suggested that I sell my books after the talk, so any sales would be my compensation. I spent time preparing my speech and practicing it, and then showed up after work at 7 p.m. one evening at a nearby office building to give my workshop to about thirty young professionals.

The workshop seemed to go well, and the audience asked good questions about where to invest and how much to save. They clapped when it was over and, though they seemed appreciative of my efforts— the host gave me a box of chocolates as a thank you—no one bought a single book. As I carted my bag of books back out to my car, exhausted after a long day and missing my daughter, I thought: Why am I doing this? Why did I agree to spend hours preparing for and giving this talk, and give up time with Kareena, when I didn't really get anything out of the exchange? Sure, I love spreading financial literacy, and it feels good to be helping people, but that work was starting to come at too high a price to my own life.

After that night, I started saying no—not always, but much more often. I became more protective of my limited free time, and energy. When I felt really crunched, I even started saying no to some paying gigs, such as a freelance article I didn't particularly want to write, and a speaking event that would have required two days of cross-country travel. Yes, I wanted to earn more money, but I also needed to protect something more valuable—my time. Instead of earning $500 for that article, I spent the weekend baking popovers with Kareena, relaxing with my husband, and away from my computer.

The hard part about knowing when and whether to say no is that a lot of times "yes" might be the better choice, even if it goes against your gut instincts. The first time an organization called me to ask if I could be a paid keynote speaker at an upcoming event, I wanted to hang up the phone and hide under a blanket. While it came with a healthy paycheck, it required three things that terrified me: flying (I get nervous), leaving my daughter for the weekend (separation anxiety applies more to me than to her), and speaking in front of a large group of people. But sometimes doing the things we're afraid of is the only way to move forward, and I'm so glad I said yes—I had a fabulous weekend with my sisters in San Francisco, met an amazing group of women, and felt like I helped them get on top of their money. And I brought home a paycheck that could pay for our family's beach rental that summer.

In fact, side-giggers often say that accepting even time-consuming, unpaid gigs is what allows them to build what becomes their thriving business. Ebony Utley gave free talks on race to colleagues' classrooms before making money from it; financial coach and author Glinda Bridgforth served on organizations' boards on a volunteer basis before becoming a paid board member. Douglas Lee Miller only realized that he could earn good money consulting on social media after noticing that people came to him for free advice when they tried to build their Twitter accounts.

Now, when I'm asked to give away my time for free, I try to pause before immediately agreeing to it. But I still make big mistakes when it comes to my extracurricular activities, and sometimes, that means everything comes crashing down.

TOP TAKEAWAYS

* One of the biggest challenges of building a side-gig is making time for it. Successful side-giggers often rely on specific strategies, such as taking advantage of lunch breaks or waking up before dawn.

* Finding a side-gig that is powered by the experience and skills gained at a full-time job, without conflicting with it, can also generate significant time efficiencies.

* When the side-gig doesn't overlap with full-time work, then side-giggers often find other ways to turn their outside pursuits into assets for their full-time employers.

* If the side-gig is totally unrelated, then a strict schedule that keeps the two activities separate can be the best policy.

* Saying no to activities and requests that don't support your priorities is an essential skill that can free up hours of time.

CHAPTER

7

Dust Yourself Off

AS I WAS SPREADING THE WORD ABOUT MY PLANNERS, I DID A POD-
cast with a local yoga studio owner, whom I'll call Carol. I've taken
classes at her studio for years, and also follow her blog, since she often
writes about creativity and setting big goals, two areas that interest
me.

For about thirty minutes, we had a lively conversation about how
to get financially organized, steps to take to save more, and how to
start saving for retirement. When it was over, we started chatting
about what else we've each been up to. I mentioned the financial
workshops that I'd started giving, and she said she'd love to host me
at her studio, since she regularly offers workshops related to life
improvement topics. I eagerly agreed—since her clientele is largely
made up of ambitious young professionals, it seemed like my perfect
audience.

I spent weeks preparing for the workshop. I picked up supplies,
including markers and construction paper, for participants to create
vision boards of their ideal spending patterns, and planned out other
exercises, related to setting big goals and then coming up with smaller
steps to work toward them.

Finally, the big day came. I went straight from work to the yoga studio, with all my supplies in hand. As I walked into the studio as a teacher for the first time, I felt my stomach flip, but I also felt prepared. One of the other yoga teachers walked me up the two flights of stairs to the third-floor studio, where the late-evening sun streamed through the windows, heating the room. I started to sweat.

Slowly, participants started trickling in, including Carol. We introduced ourselves, I passed out the worksheets, and we got started. We created visual budget maps together, to identify our spending priorities and reflect on how they lined up with our actual expenditures. We brainstormed and shared our biggest financial goals. We talked about ways to break those goals into smaller steps to make them more manageable. And we discussed strategies almost everyone can benefit from, including paying off expensive debt, saving one-quarter of one's income, and getting help from professionals when you need it.

As I got ready to lead the group through the last exercises, I checked the clock. Only forty-five minutes had passed. The workshop had been scheduled for an hour and a half. I slowed down, tried to take some yogic breaths, and continued, taking time to fully answer all the questions that came up.

A steamy hour after we began (the sun continued to shine right through the windows, even as it set), I concluded the formal part of the workshop and thanked everyone for coming, and explained that I would be sticking around to discuss individual issues and questions. Carol put her hand up. "This workshop was supposed to be ninety minutes long," she said, scrunching up her nose in clear disappointment.

My heart dropped. I had messed up, and Carol had publicly called me out on it. I had failed to deliver what had been promised to these dozen participants, each of whom paid about $30 to be there. I had embarrassed myself in front of this yoga studio owner, whom I admire and strive to emulate in many ways. And, perhaps worst of all, I had revealed that maybe I wasn't really so good at this workshop thing, after all.

At that moment, I apologized and said it had moved more quickly than I thought, but I hoped to use the remaining time in a useful way by working individually with everyone who came. Carol just nodded. I limped through the remainder of our time, answering questions about where to invest and whether to rollover retirement accounts, but inside, I felt utterly deflated. I drove home questioning my overall plan to earn a side income through my personal finance expertise and wondering about the value I could truly bring to people.

Those thoughts continued to simmer over the next few days. I sent Carol a thank-you note, and she wrote a polite email back. I wasn't sure whether to apologize. She sent the check in the mail and again I felt guilty. Did I deserve to earn $115 when I had clearly disappointed people? The experience sent me back to square one, and I started wondering whether I needed a new side-gig plan altogether.

LEARNING FROM FAILURE

Ben Popken's moment of rock-bottom clarity came when he got unexpectedly laid off from Consumerist.com, the site he had spent six years building. Luckily, Ben, now in his early thirties, was somewhat prepared, thanks to the prevailing attitude among his generation that no job is permanent. "Anyone, after six years of doing the same job, starts thinking, 'What's my future?' and making preparations. In the last year, I realized I needed to have something besides Consumerist happening for me. I started up my blog and made sure I had an established presence, so people knew where to find me," he says. He also started putting more energy into his second passion, improv comedy, by taking classes at the Upright Citizens Brigade Theater, in New York, where he lives.

That preparation paid off. Within minutes of Tweeting a link to his final "goodbye" post on Consumerist, an editor contacted him about a freelance gig. From there, Ben built his freelance and improv careers side by side. His comedy website, benpopkenisjustkidding. com, features a goofy-looking photo of himself along with funny observations and comedic videos he's made. In one, he plays the role of a newscaster and argues for melting down copper and paying off U.S. debt to China with the proceeds. (It includes a riff on the productivity of drug addicts and is much funnier than I'm making it sound.) Eventually, he might overlay advertising on the videos and promote them on youtube.com to earn money. Meanwhile, his journalism website, benpopkenwrites.com, features a much more serious-looking photo and hosts his latest consumer reporting.

Despite the divergence of his two pursuits, he moves seamlessly between the two: On a typical weekday, he wakes up around 7 a.m., makes a big cup of coffee, and sits down to start writing either comedy sketches, a blog post for his own Tumblr site, or a freelance article—"whatever seems most important and urgent," says Ben. He typically spends a few hours each week practicing and performing with his improv group, the Thesaurus Ninjas. They practice long-form improv, which means they take suggestions from the audience and then create twenty minutes of scenes that "have never been seen before and will never be seen again."

While Ben dreams of eventually becoming a comedy writer for a show or getting paid for his sketch comedy another way, for now the work is giving a boost to the rest of his life and career. Improv, he says, helps him learn how to be in the moment, how to interview people, and how to think on his feet—all valuable skills for journalists, too. "I had lost touch with some of those interpersonal skills, so in a lot of ways improv has been helpful in retraining me how to be a human. It's like the cheapest therapy out there," he jokes. "I'm more comfortable being interviewed and more comfortable talking to new people and being in the rat-tat-tat of conversational flow."

Like so many people who have experienced what feels like crushing disappointment at the time, Ben is now grateful for losing his job. "Getting laid off was the best thing that ever happened to me," he says. It forced him to question his self-worth, evaluate where he was and where he wanted to go, and to make conscious decisions about his work instead of coasting along his well-worn path. He can now pour his energy into building his improv skills and taking on new freelance assignments. "It was really an unexpected gift," he says.

Another person has also invited me to watch his stumbles and failures closeup: my father. From the outside, my dad can be intimidatingly successful: His wildlife films have won many awards, including an Oscar nomination and Emmys—and they've helped spread the message about the importance of protecting the environment. He's made IMAX films on whales, worked with celebrities like Isabella Rossellini and Alicia Silverstone, and founded an environmental film center at American University. Earlier in his career, he served in the British Navy as a mechanical engineer and, shortly before becoming an American citizen, worked on Capitol Hill and for the Environmental Protection Agency during the Carter Administration. But everything doesn't always go his way, and to me, as I deal with my own setbacks, that has been reassuring.

At some point in his fifties, my dad decided he wanted to explore a new career—that of a stand-up comic. He had long admired comedians like Jay Leno and Jerry Seinfeld, pouring over the books they wrote and studying their performances religiously. One of his own earliest and fondest childhood memories involved making his family of six roar with laughter. When he was four years old, he heard his mother wonder out loud how many famous people there were in the world. "I sat down, put my hand under my chin in a 'thinking' pose, feigned all the seriousness I could muster, and said, 'Well let's see now. First, we have Sir Winston Churchill...,'" my dad recalls. His family cracked up.

My dad had never previously pursued comedy as anything other than a hobby (and as the frequent instigator of practical jokes) though, because he was too busy building his environmental film career, teaching film students, and raising his family of three daughters. But at fifty-seven, after I brought home a brochure from a local writers' center, he decided it was time. He signed up for a six-week local stand-up class and started brainstorming funny ideas.

He invited my mom and sisters to watch his final class, which involved a performance at a local bar. As soon as I saw the venue—cheesy Hawaiian decorations, dirty floor, Christmas lights—I wanted to run back to my car. The first performer, who joked about defecation, the size of his private parts, and his lack of a sex life, only reinforced that flight instinct. I could barely look at my mom as we listened to a diatribe filled with such vulgarity it wouldn't even have been appropriate for HBO.

Then my dad was up. He sounded like a British Mister Rogers compared to the previous acts. A lot of his material was about my sisters and me: "Over the years, we've had many boys come to the house to take our daughters out on dates. Watching your daughter go out with a boy is like giving a da Vinci painting to a monkey." And: "My wife and I are always showing photos of our daughters to friends. I notice that my daughters never show their friends photos of us."

The only problem? No one laughed. Okay, some people laughed. But the bathroom jokes of the previous performers seemed to garner a much more energetic response.

That didn't stop my dad. After his class, he continued to hone his routine, regularly performing at a dive bar in Washington, D.C., and then convincing a local hotel to begin hosting comedy night every Saturday. He even got paid, between $50 and $100 a night depending on the size of the audience, and he earned every penny: He devoted much of his weekend to tinkering with his jokes and practicing them on my mom. And he continued to be the most wholesome act on stage. From what I could tell, that was only hurting him. Raunchiness, apparently, is what people want from their comedians.

After four years of regular Saturday performances and serving as master of ceremonies, my dad received an email from the manager of the event, informing him that the club would no longer need his talents; they would instead opt to hire professional comedians. My dad was hurt, and a little angry. He'd spent years of his own time and resources promoting and building the show.

He sent an email to my sisters and me telling us what happened. "This is a blow!" he wrote. "When his email first arrived this morning, I felt let down." But he quickly changed tactics, focusing instead on what he could take away from the experience, and the benefits of it ending: "This may be a blessing in disguise. I'm glad to have the extra time to put into writing my book, and strategically I'm probably wiser to focus more on giving speeches rather than doing stand-up. The typical audience at comedy clubs is not 'my' audience, compared, say, to the audience at a film conference or big dinner."

He ended up doing just that. He redoubled his efforts on the book he had long wanted to write, *Shooting in the Wild*, about the ethics of wildlife filmmaking, and found a publisher in Sierra Club books. He gave more speeches at big events in the filmmaking industry, earning a reputation as a dynamic, entertaining, and even humorous speaker. (He didn't use the exact same jokes from his stand-up routine, but many of the same principles, such as surprising and engaging the audience, applied.) In fact, he found speech-giving more satisfying than stand-up comedy, largely because he was so good at connecting with his audiences, who were always eager to learn from him.

Now, he says, he looks back on his brief stand-up career with great fondness. "I learned a lot about performing on stage, which helps me in my speaking and teaching. And it gave me the chance to study comedy and joke-telling, skills that are important to me in all the endeavors in my life," he says. While he failed at his goal of performing on a regional or national stage—preferably Jay Leno's—he succeeded at trying for one of his long-time goals. And he's proud that for four years, he worked, and was even paid, to be a comic.

CHANGING COURSE

Many of the side-giggers I interviewed described similar moments of utter dejection and failure, and those disappointments often allowed (or forced) their side-gigs to change directions and ultimately flourish. When Tory Johnson was laid off from her dream television job at the start of her career, as described in Chapter 1, she vowed never to be so dependent on a single employer ever again. That commitment led to her now-successful company, Women for Hire. Amy Stringer-Mowat of Chapter 2 was an underemployed architect when she posted her cutting board inventions on Etsy on a whim. Chapter 6's Jessi Baden-Campbell was unable to make a living as an opera singer when she found financial stability in a full-time job that allowed her to sing outside of it. Alisha Williams failed to make it to the 2008 Olympic trials, which inspired her to get a new coach, follow a new training regime, and discover that she was iron-deficient. Jeffrey Nash, inventor of the Juppy, was crushed when his long-time employer cut his salary, but that's what motivated him to create the briskly selling Juppy.

What they have in common is resilience, and a determination to find a way to move past what can seem, at the time, like a crushing setback. They used the occasion to motivate them to try even harder, or to try something different. And that's usually the difference between those who find success in their side-gigs and those who don't: Those who do simply never gave up.

Finding that bottomless source of motivation partly depends on choosing well in the first place. The side-pursuit has to be something that you're so in love with that you would do it even if no one was paying you. It should energize you so much that you want to keep going, even when all signs seem to be telling you to stop. Successful side-giggers pause to recalibrate, slightly alter their direction, and then keep going.

Still, it's not easy. Here are seven strategies side-giggers employ to find motivation amid disappointment:

► **Turn to your online community for support.** Do the people you follow online ever share their own failures? I was comforted after reading career author Emily Bennington's blog post about her own disastrous speaking event. "Yesterday morning I delivered what I considered to be one of the top three worst presentations of my career," she wrote, adding that it was for her largest client. She felt "humiliated, disappointed, angry, sad, confused, second-guessing everything, and—frankly—a little shocked." Just knowing that I'm not the only one to flop in front of an audience was reassuring.

► **Think about the fact that the most successful people fail.** It happened to Jennifer Lopez and Ben Affleck with *Gigli*. Best-selling author Emily Giffin, who worked as a lawyer when she started writing her first young adult novel, was rejected by publishers before landing multi-book deals. Jennifer Weiner says she queried twenty-five agents for what became her bestseller *Good in Bed*, and that she received twenty-four rejections. At the 2008 Beijing Olympics, hurdler Lolo Jones stumbled over one of the final hurdles, ruining her chance to medal. She bounced back to come in a close fourth in London in 2012. The most successful people in your own field have almost certainly experienced setbacks, and with a little Internet research, you might be able to get the details.

▶ **Make a plan B.** Even just jotting down notes on what you will do if plan A fails to materialize can ease anxiety over a potentially dismal outcome. Katy Gathright knows that if Designed Good doesn't work out, she'll look for an editorial position in San Francisco, or return to the novel she started writing last year. CommonPlace founder Peter Davis says he would look for a public policy position in Washington, D.C.—something that would allow him to continue working on civic issues.

▶ **Discover what makes you feel better.** For April Bowles Olin of Blacksburg Belle, it's thinking about all the times she heard "yes" instead of "no," and then simply "getting right back up on the horse, instead of moping." Other people, myself included, like to mope for a bit, preferably with trashy reality TV and ice cream in hand, before continuing on. Common tricks also include calling your mom, buying a latte, and reading negative reviews of best-selling books to realize you're not the only one who deals with negative feedback.

▶ **Ignore the haters.** If it's mean Tweeters, anonymous comments, or negative online reviews that are getting you down, then just consider that the attention also means you have achieved some level of success.

▶ **Know that you'll probably end up thinking it was for the best.** Psychologist Dan Gilbert has found that as a species, we aren't so good at predicting our future emotional state. We think negative experiences will ruin us, when in reality, we have a remarkable ability to make the best of whatever happens. Applied to side-gigs, that suggests that even if we experience failure, we will be okay, as Ben Popken, my dad, and I learned.

► **Just keep going.** That's all you can do—make some tweaks, respond to any feedback as necessary, and keep on trying. Pandora founder Tim Westergren has talked openly about how the company struggled to get financing in its early years, when he pitched over 300 venture capital firms. But he kept going, working for no pay, and the company took off. It eventually went public, valued at over $3 billion.

After my own workshop debacle, I, too, shifted gears. After much introspection, I realized that I did want to continue speaking to groups, but I wanted to do it better. I rewrote my workshop and speech template to add more stories and details, so my future talks would never run the risk of ending early again. Before my next event, which was at an event cosponsored by a local credit union, newspaper, and university, I spent extra time preparing and practicing, and gave the audience useful strategies that they could bring home with them. Attendees came up to me afterwards with more questions, and I felt that I had actually helped some of them.

Most importantly, I didn't let that one workshop flop derail me. In fact, my speaking gigs started becoming a bigger part of my side-career, and in some ways, the part where I feel most useful to people.

TOP TAKEAWAYS

* Failure is an inevitable part of any side-gig pursuit, and learning how to bounce back is essential for success.

* Strategies for resilience vary widely by individual, but include taking a break, getting perspective, trying a new approach, or simply carrying on.

CHAPTER

8

Karma

JOHN TULLOCK FIRST DISCOVERED HIS SIDE INCOME IN THE FORM of violet Virginia bluebells, which are native to his Knoxville, Tennessee, home. The luminescent, bell-shaped flowers were easy for him to grow in his backyard garden, and also easy to sell to local garden centers, which have trouble keeping bluebells and other popular native plants in stock. He soon expanded into poppies, bleeding hearts, trilliums, and orchids. A community relations manager for the local Barnes & Noble, John spent his weekends tending to his garden and packaging up the flowers for sale. Each season, he made around $10,000 in profit, which he shared with his gardening partner.

For John, now in his early sixties, earning a healthy side income from his hobby wasn't enough. He also wanted to share his knowledge with other would-be growers. "I know in the tough economic times we've had, a lot of folks have been looking for ways to make extra money. This is not rocket science, especially with wild flowers. I like the idea of helping people and giving them a little bit of direction," he says. That's why he writes his blog, The New American Homestead (johntullock.blogspot.com), and published a book, *Pay Dirt: How to Make $10,000 a Year from Your Backyard Garden.*

He started writing about gardening just as Americans were hungriest for the information. When the recession took over in 2008 and 2009, more people started looking for ways not only to save money, but also to invest in their homes and embrace a do-it-yourself culture. Even people without spacious yards found ways to join the trend: The American Community Gardening Association estimates that there are around 18,000 community gardens in the United States and Canada. When I looked for one to visit myself, I discovered that I unknowingly passed one every day on the way to pick up my daughter from pre-school. On a recent commute, I stopped by for a brief self-guided tour. The smell of vine-ripe tomatoes hit me first. Rows of carefully tended gardens, filled with cantaloupes, beefsteak tomatoes, eggplant, and Swiss chard, each one no bigger than a Jacuzzi.

While many people simply grow for themselves and their families, others, like John, opt to earn a small side income by selling the fruits of their labor to local farmers' markets, small grocers, or gardening centers. John's advice for fellow gardeners, based on his own experience, includes focusing on flowers and vegetables that are easy to grow and popular locally. As he discovered, "It wasn't the weird and unusual ones that are good sellers." He also prefers to work with local garden centers rather than deal with the hassle of packaging orders to mail to customers who live farther away. "The volume didn't justify that extra trouble," he says. As a result of sharing his hard-earned expertise through his writing, he's made friends around the world and is often asked to speak to local groups about building backyard gardens. Like computer programmers who dedicate hours to writing open source code or photographers who share their work publicly through Creative Commons licensing, John helps others by sharing his knowledge and expertise.

Giving a hand to other people trying to tackle the same overwhelming challenge of launching a side-gig comes naturally to many side-giggers, especially those who have already achieved some degree of success. This isn't a community shaped by a competitive or "mean girls" spirit; in fact, quite the opposite. Side-giggers often share ideas, resources, and even work.

When Joe Cain, the founder of sidegig.com profiled in Chapter 1, needed help with his website, he hired a web designer who had just started his own tech support side-business. When jewelry designer Erica Sara from Chapter 4 needed marketing assistance, she decided to work with Megan Moynihan Callaway, the public relations professional who was just starting to build her own brand outside of her corporate agency. It was more affordable than hiring a full-fledged company, but more importantly, she felt that Megan understood what she needed, and understood her business.

Alexis Grant, a friend and former coworker who launched her social media consulting business on the side, now employs a handful of young people with full-time jobs who are also trying to build their side-businesses as social media experts or writers. "I don't specifically look to hire other side-giggers, but it does end up happening," she says, partly because she usually finds her hires through Twitter or her newsletter and blog, and many of the people who follow her are interested in building side-gigs. (One of her most popular e-books, which she sells through her website, alexisgrant.com, is on how to build a part-time social media business.)

Alexis likes working with side-giggers, she says, because "they tend to be go-getters—ambitious people working toward their dreams. They're smart and reliable but still learning the ropes. Not only do I enjoy helping these go-getters learn, but they also tend to be more affordable and perhaps more gung-ho than people who have already figured out how to make a full-time living off their passion."

MAKING A DIFFERENCE

As they become more financially secure and confident in their success, many side-giggers add more explicit "giving back" components to their side-businesses, as a way of helping others while still building their own financial security. That's why Martin Cody of Cellar Angels (from Chapter 6) allows customers to select the charity of their choice to receive a portion of wine sale proceeds. And why Chris Guillebeau, the travel blogger and author of *The Art of Non-Conformity*, encouraged attendees of his World Domination Summit conference in July

2012 to "donate their birthdays" to an organization called charity: water, a nonprofit that brings clean drinking water to communities in developing countries. (Donating your birthday means asking friends to donate instead of buying you a gift.)

For some side-giggers, though, the drive to give back in some way is so central to their original motivation that their pursuits are rooted in public service from the start. Asher Corson first became president of his neighborhood's civic association when he was a junior in college. Residents of his neighborhood, the historic Foggy Bottom in Washington, D.C., home to the Watergate and State Department, often found themselves clashing with the large university in their midst, George Washington, where Asher was a student. As he learned more about local politics and met local residents, he discovered that they felt the head of the neighborhood commission at the time was hard to reach, and didn't help them navigate local issues or effectively express their concerns about the growth of the university. "They asked me to run against her. I was young, energetic, and very involved in student politics, and this offered me the chance to run for a position in D.C. government."

Asher ran, and won by a landslide. He immediately got to work on several hot-button neighborhood issues, including creating a fund to rebuild and provide ongoing maintenance of the local library by allowing a developer to use the space above the library. "We not only got a brand-new library out of this deal, but we got something no other library or neighborhood in D.C. has ever had—a dedicated revenue stream to maintain our library," he says.

While time-consuming—Asher estimates he spends between ten and twenty-five hours a month on his commissioner work—the position doesn't pay, at least not in cash. Instead, Asher has been able to use the part-time position to shape his career. Now entering his thirties, his neighborhood position led him to a full-time job working for a member of the city council as director of communities. Today, as he builds his own public relations firm, he has deep connections and roots in the community, largely from his political work. (Local public servants often juggle two jobs, since the pay for such positions tends to range from zero to low, especially in small towns. The recent mayor of Herndon, Virginia, a position that pays $6,000 a year, works primarily as a personal trainer, for example.)

Other public service side-gigs start with more entrepreneurial impulses: When Emily Kaminski was pregnant with her son in 2009, she came down with an infection that required an anti-fungal cream. When she went to pick it up at the pharmacy, she discovered it was $55, despite what she thought was good insurance coverage. Instead of just paying for the medicine, she called around to other pharmacies, and found that the price varied widely, and even went as low as $18 at a nearby Costco. "Since I had to fill it twice, that was a big savings," says Emily, a stay-at-home mom in Atlanta.

That discovery gave her an idea: What if she started a website that allowed people to easily compare drug prices at local pharmacies, so they could simply pick up their prescriptions where it costs the least? With her background in education and her husband's experience in the tech world, Emily developed her idea and submitted it to a pitch session sponsored by a local business. She didn't win, but got a lot of valuable feedback that helped her shape the concept. She hired a freelancer to build the website, design a logo, and launch frugalpharmacies.com. She started reading up on financial and health blogs so she could more easily answer visitors' questions and offer background information, such as the meaning of co-pays and deductibles. She collected pricing information by calling pharmacies and asking users to submit information.

Soon after launching, she discovered an audience eager for the kind of information she was providing, and her site now gets over a thousand visitors a month, largely from search engines. "From a consumer's perspective, it's a really cumbersome process to go ahead and figure out what the price should be on any particular medication. With milk, you know the general prices, but I don't shop enough for medications to know. This area is lacking a lot of transparency," she says. She acknowledges that price isn't the most important factor when it comes to medication, but that it's an essential component of the overall discussion. As she's done more research and added more medications to her site, she's found that many drugs vary by as much as $40 or $50, depending on which pharmacy you visit.

Muddying up the comparison process is insurance, since coverage varies by person and medication. At frugalpharmacies.com, Emily displays the price customers pay without insurance, to allow for apples-to-apples comparisons. She says that approach is also more useful for people with high deductibles.

Emily is still working out how to turn this idea into a self-sustaining, or even profitable, website. Her ideas include creating a donate button on the site, partnering with an organization such as a patient-advocacy group, or developing a mobile app. For now, she's just glad to feel like she's helping people who can least afford their medication. One site visitor, a cancer survivor, contacted her about a medication that his doctor prescribed for arterial health. It cost him $109 a month, and because the insurer only covered a limited number of pills, he went without the medication altogether for long periods of time. But because Walmart and Target were currently offering the medication at a discount, Emily was able to help him cut his costs by more than half. "When you're sick, you don't have time to call around looking," she says.

Mark Wilson, a technology writer now in his early thirties, had a similar moment when he realized he could start something that helped people. In 2010, while he was working for the website Gizmodo as a senior editor, he started thinking about the next stage of his career. "I realized, I hate reading the news, it feels like everything is so bad and frustrating, and there's nothing I can do about it." Mark, who lives in Chicago, started wondering if there was, in fact, a way he could make an impact, by giving money to groups that were trying to solve pressing global problems. "I went to give money, and I thought, 'This is a horrible experience. I don't know what I care about most—funding cancer research, supporting human rights—I care about them all.'" That's when he came up with the idea for Philanthroper.com, a site that would allow people to give small amounts, as little as $1 a day, to good causes, and make a difference through their combined efforts. The idea, loosely modeled on Groupon, is to leverage the power of social media. "I thought about how this model of spending really appeals to people, and how you could reframe it around doing good. There's a $1 store, and McDonald's has a $1 menu. It's easy to spend $1 on a whim," he says.

In January 2011, after leaving Gizmodo to freelance, he used his savings to launch the site, along with a coder and design firm. Soon, the site had 1,000 beta users, which then grew to 8,500 subscribers, many of whom came through social media outreach. Mark and his team vetted nonprofits thoroughly before featuring them as a "daily deal." Over the next year and a half, the site raised almost $180,000 for charity.

Mark and his team ruled out taking a cut of the donations to fund the site, and instead considered advertising or a subscription-based model. But because they were growing linearly, and not exponentially, they had a hard time monetizing it in a way that would allow the site to sustain itself. Eventually, they decided to sell the site, and are currently talking with celebrities, nonprofits, and businesses who are interested. "A lot of people want to run it, but I'm more interested in making sure whoever takes it over is more capable than my team," he says. He thinks that with the right support and aggressive marketing, it could really take off. As for his own career, Mark landed a full-time job at *Fast Company*, where he interviews other entrepreneurs about their start-ups. He says, "I'm glad I tried to build a product on my own—I understand what it takes to manage a team, get talent to work together, and how simple things can be complicated underneath." That experience now informs his reporting.

Peter Davis, founder of CommonPlace, the website that helps neighbors engage with each other featured in Chapter 5, is also driven by a larger purpose—building meaningful communities for people. He was inspired by Robert Putnam, author of *Bowling Alone* and a political scientist at Harvard, who writes about the decline of communities in America. In *Bowling Alone*, Putnam argues that not only is the sense of community declining, but that its presence is absolutely essential, and leads to less crime, better health, and more trust. Peter wants to help reverse the trend and make communities strong again.

"We want to build that third space where people meet and get together. So many websites online aren't meaningful at all and are just trying to distract away our time. It's refreshing to work on something that really has a cause," says Peter.

For Jason Nicholas, a veterinarian in Portland, Oregon, the cause is spreading information to pet owners about how to keep their pets safe from common household dangers. While working as a resident in emergency and critical care at an animal hospital, he realized that most injured pets shouldn't have gotten hurt in the first place. "So much of what my colleagues and I were seeing was preventable. It hit me that I could use the Internet and outreach to increase people's awareness. There hasn't been a push to increase awareness among pet owners other than the importance of vaccinating and heartworm prevention," he says. "For example, every dog owner should know about the dangers of xylitol, a sweetener used in sugar-free gum, toothpaste, and other popular products," says Jason. "If a 100-pound Rottweiler eats a pack of sugar-free gum, they're probably going to die." While xylitol is safe for people, it's toxic to dogs, and can causes seizures, comas, and liver failure. Similarly, certain types of lilies are poisonous to cats, a fact that many cat owners do not know. Even small steps, such as hanging bags on sturdy hooks out of reach of pets, can help avoid poisonings.

To spread information about pet safety, Jason, now forty, launched his website, thepreventivevet.com, which offers pet-proofing guides for every room of the house, as well as a blog with infographics on heat stroke and other common dangers. He also got to work on two in-depth books on cat and dog safety, each containing 101 tips for pet owners. He hired an illustrator and designer to help make them easy to read, and wants to eventually get them into every vet office and animal shelter in the country.

At first, Jason spent his own time and money without much compensation, other than the knowledge that he was helping prevent pet injuries. He scaled back his clinic hours so he worked three days a week, and spent the rest of his time building his website (along with raising his two young daughters). He also invested between $20,000 and $25,000 of his own money to get his website and books off the ground. Now, he's starting to look for more ways to make sure his pet safety campaign can pay for itself and turn into a sustainable project. He recently started working one on one with new pet owners, to help them pet-proof their homes, and launched a campaign on the crowdfunding site Indiegogo.com to raise funds to publish his books. (Two weeks into the campaign, he's raised over $5,000.) "My naive goal is to sell lots of copies and make the money back," he says. (He's also dedicating a portion of proceeds to dog and cat charities.) His project could lead to other potential revenue streams down the road, too, such as teaching pet safety classes or working with pet insurance companies on education programs.

Top Resources for Crowd-Funding

When you're pursuing a side-gig with the primary goal of "doing good," the method of creating financial sustainability is not always obvious. But thanks to the boom in crowd-funding websites, it's easier than ever to find support. Here are some of the most popular sites:

Crowdtilt.com: Users can start campaigns for almost anything, from charitable goals to vacation rentals, and then raise money from their friends and extended networks. Unlike other crowd-funding sites, most campaigns are private.

Indiegogo.com: One of the most popular sites, indiegogo.com features creative projects alongside education and political campaigns. It's easy to upload your video and tell your story.

Kickstarter.com: People raise money for creative pursuits from film projects to technology ideas. (Unlike other sites, posters don't get any of the money unless they reach their target amount, and projects must be approved before they are posted.)

Rockethub.com: This site connects "creatives," who it defines as anyone seeking funding to develop work, with "fuelers," who contribute money to those projects.

StartSomeGood.com: This site lets social entrepreneurs launch and raise money for their campaigns. The only catch is that the project must do some form of "social good," as the website puts it.

NONPROFIT SIDE-GIGS

Nonprofits dedicated to charitable causes are often routed in entrepreneurial impulses as well. Angele "AJ" Thomas got the idea for her nonprofit, the Infuse Program Foundation, when she was mentoring students at an inner-city high school in San Jose, California, in 2009. AJ, who at twenty-seven is a full-time program manager for new product introduction at a large tech company in Silicon Valley, realized that the students she was mentoring could benefit so much from the entrepreneurial energy and resources of their city. "They had less of an opportunity to take advantage of the same opportunities that somebody on the west side could—somebody who had parents working at a high-tech company," she says. "I said, 'We need to democratize the energy of Silicon Valley.'"

In an effort to do that, AJ started talking with local executives, both inside her own company and at others. "I got our executives to buy into the vision of what I was trying to do. They share the same values of equalizing education and supporting the educational community," she says. Her company appointed her as its educational ambassador, which meant she started attending Silicon Valley educational meetings on its behalf, which also helped her build her nonprofit.

Under the umbrella of her nonprofit, she organizes after-school programs on entrepreneurship, taught by members of the local Silicon Valley community, including herself. The classes culminate in a pitch session to local executives, who award internships and scholarships based on the students' ideas and presentations. One winner now has a patent pending for a product that serves as a coffee cupholder, slap bracelet, and watch. Another graduate of the program is currently majoring in chemical engineering at University of California, Davis.

While AJ doesn't get directly paid for her work on Infuse, she points to many ways that she benefits: Her company sees her as a leader as a result of her educational work. She occasionally gives paid speeches to other tech companies about corporate social responsibility and how to apply entrepreneurial principles to one's job. But the biggest payment, by far, is what AJ calls the fulfillment factor. "Having kids say, 'I can do this, I can go to college,' and spreading that entrepreneurial mindset to these kids so they start thinking about other opportunities, too, and seeing them light up . . . being able to bring that into focus for them," she says, is what keeps her going. The Infuse Program has now taught almost 200 students in two schools, a number she plans to soon expand.

Meredith Alexander, founder of the nonprofit Milk + Bookies, describes her own payoff in similar terms. I first discovered her organization as I was looking for birthday party ideas for Kareena, who was about to turn two. Anyone who has young children knows that expectations for birthday parties these days can be high: Lavish goodie bags, paid entertainers, and commercial venues, such as gyms complete with trampolines and zip lines, are now the norm in some social circles. As a relatively new mom, I was overwhelmed, and not sure where to start.

In my online search for ideas, I discovered Milk + Bookies. I had to learn more, so I gave Meredith a call. As a floral-designer-turned-full-time mom in Santa Monica, she found herself searching for ways to spend meaningful family time together. She also wanted her three-year-old to start to grasp the concept of public service. So she arranged for a local bookstore to host a group of her friends with small children on a Sunday. The children picked out their favorite books to donate to another child locally, personalized them with bookplate inscriptions, and snacked on milk and cookies along the way. "The line at the check-out counter was a thirty-minute wait—that's when I knew I was onto something, and that other parents were also looking for these kinds of meaningful activities," says Meredith.

So she got to work creating a model that could be replicated by other parents looking for book giving–themed birthday parties or scout troop projects for their children. In 2008, she officially formed a nonprofit and brought in two of her friends with fundraising and financial experience to serve on the board. Together, they developed and spread the concept, selling "bookies boxes" on the website, milkandbookies.org, complete with bookmarks, balloons, and stickers, to make it easy for parents to host events at their house, or any other location they chose. Instead of gifts, party guests bring a copy of their favorite book to donate to a local nonprofit, school, or library. (Proceeds from the bookies box sales go to materials; the nonprofit supports itself, including two staff member positions, from donations.)

"It's amazing to see the reaction from parents. They breathe a sigh of relief when they find a model that's already completely set up for them. All they have to do is show up with the cake," says Meredith, who's now in her early forties. Her favorite part is the impact she sees Milk + Bookies having on children: "We are really excited about the idea of switching these young kids on to how great it feels to give back, and we hope they go out and recreate that for themselves in all different ways. We're raising a generation of problem-solvers, do-ers, and givers," she says.

Those terms also describe Tracey Webb, who started Black Benefactors, a giving circle based in the Washington, D.C., area. A giving circle, Tracey explains, is essentially a group of people who get together to jointly donate money to causes they care about. "The fact that it's collective, that makes a bigger impact," she explains. Webb, who's in her forties, decided to form the circle on top of her full-time job writing grants for nonprofits after noticing that many small nonprofits were hungry for more resources to complete their missions. They needed staff training, help developing their boards, and technical assistance, too.

So Tracey created a giving circle that raises money to support the operations of nonprofits with budgets under $500,000. Since donors often specify that their gifts go only toward programs, it was important for Tracey to specify that the money could be used to run the nonprofits—the area of weakness where she thought they needed the most help. Members of her giving circle not only donate money (at least $250 a year each), but they also often share their expertise, in management, board development, or web development. The group, made up primarily of African Americans in their thirties through sixties, typically donates at least $10,000 a year to local groups. It's been so successful that Tracey plans to soon launch a new group, the Young

Black Benefactors, to attract a younger demographic to local philanthropy.

As Tracey and all of the side-giggers profiled in this chapter discovered, dedicating time to public service or a charity doesn't have to mean financial sacrifice—just the opposite. Even if the pursuit itself doesn't come with a salary, it often leads to greater connections, resources, and richer experiences, all of which can boost a career, life goals, and overall financial picture. Most meaningfully, perhaps, it can help lead to bigger plans and goals down the road, as side-giggers prepare for their futures.

TOP TAKEAWAYS

* Side-giggers often help each other, by sharing information, connections, and advice. They also frequently hire each other.

* Some side-giggers are originally motivated by the desire to make a difference, and they build their businesses around this goal.

CHAPTER
9

Endgame

WHEN I ASKED PEOPLE ABOUT THEIR LONG-TERM SIDE-GIG GOALS, they often said that they just wanted more of what they already had: a full-time job that provides a stable home base while they experiment and expand on the side. "I really enjoy what I do during the day. I love art, I love technical stuff," says singer Corinne Delaney from Chapter 6. She has no plans to ever leave her day job.

Chapter 3's tax guru Jason Malinak gave a similar response. "I'm happy, and I love my job. I consider my passion my career and my Etsy shop my hobby," he says. Still, he adds, he intends to continue growing his customer base as much as possible.

Sydney Owen, the skydiver and career coach from Chapter 3, plans to continue jumping and coaching indefinitely. So too does writer and law office manager Jennifer Teates (Chapter 6), who gets her writing ideas from her day job. Martin Cody (Chapter 6) also wants to continue building his online wine business on one computer while he takes care of his medical sales responsibilities with another. These side-giggers all found a balance between their two pursuits that is stable enough to support and fulfill them for the foreseeable future.

In the process, they are redefining financial independence. It doesn't mean bringing in a million dollars a year, or earning enough in royalties to retire to Belize at age thirty-five. Instead, it means knowing that a single boss, single employer, or single paycheck isn't the only thing keeping the bills paid each month. It means knowing at least one income stream will always be there, regardless of the economy's fluctuations or an employer's bottom line. It means knowing that we, not our employers, have ultimate control over our financial well-being.

That's why the question for many side-giggers isn't so much: "When can I leave my full-time job?" as it is: "Why would I ever want to leave my full-time job?" Full-time work offers safety and stability, in contrast to riskier after-hours entrepreneurial pursuits. In addition to a steady paycheck, my own full-time job offers retirement and health benefits, free coffee, camaraderie, tech support, and, perhaps most important, room to learn and grow within an established company. While my own side-gig is fulfilling and profitable, it could never replace all those benefits—financial, social, and emotional.

It's the combination of the full-time job and the side-gig, after all, that provides the greatest financial security. Each gives us a backup plan in case the other suddenly fails us. With only a full-time job, we are walking on a high-wire sans safety net; with just a side-gig, we can find ourselves lolling in the safety net, unable to climb to the greater heights that the connections, support, and backing of an employer can provide. As Silicon Valley tech manager and nonprofit founder AJ Thomas put it, having both a side-gig and a full-time job means "you can glide and soar, and then come back to the cliff when you need a jump."

It's hard to do both, but the alternatives— suffering through an extended layoff without a trickle of earned income, or being bored with the monotony and languishing pay of a thirty-year career—are even less appealing.

BREAKING THE FALL

Some side-giggers, though, don't have the luxury of maintaining both pursuits forever. Their side-gig income saved them when their main jobs disappeared. Cake designer Chris Furin (Chapter 1) focused on his cake business when his father's diner shut its doors. Nicole Crimaldi Emerick (Chapter 1) turned to her own side-business, Ms. Career Girl, when she was unexpectedly laid off from her start-up. Chhayal Parikh, a former coworker I wrote about in *Generation Earn*, would have suddenly lost all of her income when she got laid off from her job as a video producer had she not already been teaching fitness classes on evenings and weekends. Those classes brought her close to $10,000 a year, and when her day job disappeared, she picked up new classes to keep her solvent until she landed her next videographer job.

Indeed, the boundaries between side-gig and full-time job are increasingly fluid, and side-giggers frequently move back and forth between worlds without much difficulty. When Jeff Frederick, father of three in Troy, Michigan, got laid off from his architectural firm in 2008, he signed on to Elance.com, the freelance website, to look for project work. "I wanted to keep up my skills while I was looking for a job," he says.

Jeff soon landed work designing small projects for residential and commercial clients; one of his first jobs was designing a deck trellis for someone's backyard. "[The client] was looking for something out of the box, different from what he could find at Home Depot," says Jeff. After leaving that client a satisfied customer, he started landing more jobs through the site, including office design work for a company in Omaha. He didn't earn as much as he does when he's working full time at a firm, but he says that extra income was essential to getting his family through his layoff. On average, he earns around $50 an hour through his Elance. com work, for a total of over $10,000 since he started.

Once he found a full-time job at a different architecture firm, he didn't stop his Elance work. "I can work a couple hours a night, and over a week I can get a project done," says Jeff, who puts the extra earnings into savings and general household costs. When he got laid off a second time, he again focused on Elance.com—full time; and now that he's once again employed at a company, he continues his freelance projects on evenings and weekends. Maintaining that side-gig gives him flexibility to move between being a full-time employee, freelancer, and side-gigger with relative ease.

Other side-giggers decide to leave their jobs voluntarily. That was the case for Michael Carvin, who started working on his concept for a new personal finance tool while he was working full time in private equity. He was planning to buy his first house, and, even as someone who analyzes finances for a living, found the process extremely confusing. "I thought if anyone should understand the economics of it, it should be me, but it was enormously more complicated than I anticipated," says Michael, who's based in New York City. But with realtors urging him to consider homes that were well above the budget he felt comfortable with and multiple mortgage options, he decided he needed to build his own financial model, similar to the models he builds for companies in his day job.

As Michael created that model, which incorporates tax savings, mortgage rates, and the expected future value of real estate, among other factors, he started sharing it with friends and family members, too. That's when he realized there was a market for the kind of personalized financial guidance that his tool provided. "We had great feedback, which gave us a lot of confidence, and working on new technology in personal finance felt like a big leap forward. We felt like we could help people make big decisions," he says.

So Michael, along with his cofounder Philip Camilleri, worked on building out the model in more detail, adding detailed projections on taxes, expenses, liabilities, and income. He worked on the evenings and weekends for about eight months before deciding to leave his company. While the financial training and experience he got from his full-time work was essential to helping him build his business idea, he says, "It became obvious about two months before we quit that to take any next steps we would need to become 'full-timers'. . . . I was certainly worried about losing the financial security of being on someone's payroll, but we had exhausted what we could do while still working." The new website, SmartAsset.com, needed new business partnerships and investors. "It is hard enough to get people to take your phone call when you are just two guys in an office, but if you tell them you are moonlighting, it becomes even more difficult to be taken seriously and make important connections," says Michael.

Today, with a staff of five and coverage in major publications, including *Fast Company* and *PC World*, Michael knows he made the right decision. "If I knew then what I know now, I would have left sooner," he says. Along with his cofounder, he's expanded the site to include guidance on credit scores, retirement, and renting versus buying, and plans to expand soon to even more areas, including life insurance and investing. While initially sustained by investors, the site aims to eventually become profitable by referring people to financial products, such as mortgages, that make the most sense for them. At thirty, Michael's own financial life is looking promising: He owns his own thriving business.

Maria Sokurashvili from Chapter 4 made a similar choice when she decided to leave her information technology job to work full time on her website, dcurbanmom.com, along with her husband. Between being a mother of two, her full-time job, and her popular website, she says, "I had no extra time, so I realized the situation could not go on."

Todd Henry, the founder of The Accidental Creative from Chapter 2, says he decided to leave his full-time job as creative director at a nonprofit when he simply no longer had time for both, given the rate at which his business was growing.

For acupuncturist and therapeutic masseuse Lucinda Lyon-Vaiden (Chapter 5), time was also the deciding factor. She worked as a meeting planner during the day and holistic healer from 4:30 to 6:30 for ten years, and then realized her schedule was holding back her business. "People were disappointed; they couldn't get in, and I traveled for work sometimes and couldn't see clients. So I was happy when I could add more hours to my day," she says, which she did by quitting her day job.

Not everyone makes an either/or decision. Dana Lisa Young from Chapter 6 scaled back her content management work by moving from a full-time position to contract work, which allowed her to focus on building her holistic health business. Yoga teacher Melissa Van Orman

(Chapter 6) replaced her stressful consulting job with part-time university work to supplement her yoga income. Alexis Grant (Chapter 8) left her full-time journalism job when another company hired her to write and edit career-related content several days a week, giving her time during the rest of the week to build her own website, write digital guides, and work on her social media business. "That offer made me feel financially secure enough to go off on my own," she says.

SEEKING SATISFACTION

When I asked side-giggers what makes them feel fulfilled in their work over the long term, they almost always pointed to signs that they were making a positive impact on the world, even in some small way. For the side-giggers who launched public service pursuits, such as Emily Kaminski of frugalpharmacies.com or AJ Thomas of Infuse Program Foundation, their positive impact was obvious, but it's also apparent for many people whose primary goal is more business-oriented. While financial security usually plays a key role in why people build side-gigs, they often find a deeper payoff along the way, too, especially if they choose a pursuit that is closely aligned with their skills, values, and dreams.

As her jewelry business took off, Febe Hernandez (Chapter 3) started hiring young people from her home in the Bronx to work on her social media accounts and graphic design. When they get together, the members of "Team Febe" don T-shirts with her company's logo: "Sacrifice nothing." Helping young people is one of the most gratifying components of her business, she says, and one she plans to continue long after she retires from her career in national security.

For children's book publisher Calee Lee (Chapter 3), the satisfaction comes from passing out royalty checks to her writers and illustrators, as well as connecting young readers with new role models. "I was raised to see the value in employing others, so on some level, writing royalty checks is one of the most exciting things I do. I am building the economy on a tangible level for artists, and it's important we value artists, and give them a way to earn a living wage," she says.

Maia Heyck-Merlin, the teacher-turned-organizer from Chapter 2, says she knew she had to continue giving workshops to teachers about how to be more organized when teachers said it helped them want to stay in the classroom. Keeping teachers from quitting is a huge problem in education, and Maia feels like she's doing her part by helping them learn how to juggle messages from parents, homework assignments, and administrative tasks. "Just hearing those individual teacher stories made me feel that I had to continue," she says.

Prakash Dheeriya, a finance professor at California State University-Dominguez Hills, found a way to pass on a legacy of financial literacy through his side-gig. He started writing finance books for his two elementary-school-aged sons as a way to teach them basic money skills, such as risks and returns, opportunity costs, and credit. He thinks of it as the legacy he is leaving his children. He soon realized that other children could also benefit from the lessons, so he created a series of books that he sells through his website, finance4kidz.com.

"All we do is teach kids to save and budget, but we rarely teach them the relationship between risk and return, and then someone like Madoff comes around and says, 'Let me give you the opportunity to make tons of money.' That comes with risk. We need to teach kids that," says Prakash. He feels like he's found his calling by sharing these financial lessons, which connects his decades of experience teaching finance with the demographic that is perhaps most in need of these skills.

Melissa Van Orman, the former consultant and current yoga teacher and university instructor, gets a similar type of satisfaction from her new mix of jobs. Unlike at her consulting job, which took place in what she describes as a stressful, hostile work environment, Melissa finds her time in the yoga studio and classroom to be deeply fulfilling, largely because she can see the transformation she's helping to foster in other people's lives. Her classes are vigorous; she says her goal is to keep people fully engaged, which "helps people create distance from their mental habits and maybe create space for something new or more helpful to emerge." She achieves that effect through her instruction, voice intonation, lighting, music, and physical assists.

One of her students, whom she teaches in private sessions as well as group classes, found that yoga helped her to stop dieting and instead have a more intuitive relationship with food, which allowed her to sustain a healthy weight loss for the first time in her life. Another student decided to leave her twenty-year communications career to teach yoga full time; another went from living off of burgers and takeout to being a vegan. She's noticed similar transformations among her college students, who have switched degrees from business to public health and quit smoking. "I seek to set a supportive tone and provide resources where students feel inspired and confident to make changes on their own," she says, adding, "I view my role as creating a space people want to return to again and again—repetition is a powerful and effective way for this kind of self-reflective work to occur."

Her students are so grateful that they often leave her little gifts or thoughtful notes; her Facebook page is filled with thanks for a great class or for her "juicy assists" on the yoga mat. While she's soft-spoken, Melissa has a gentle strength and authority that comes through when she's teaching; she inspires students to push themselves just where they need to go. "Part of why I went into public health was because I wanted to make positive change in the world, and I saw people in the yoga studio making huge changes in their lives, and I was a piece of that. It's so exciting to be a part of that transformation for people."

Melissa's experience resonates with some of my favorite research on career satisfaction, which comes from Jamie Ladge, assistant professor of management and organizational development at Northeastern University's D'Amore-McKim School of Business. Instead of focusing exclusively on the financial rewards of work, she explores more subjective measures of career success, including how satisfied people say they are with their work. Satisfaction, she says, is not just about income, but about what she calls "personal rewards."

Her research can be interpreted as supporting a new, more flexible model of work that incorporates periods of work for a full-time employer, part-time work combined with a side-career, and periods of freelance or contract work only, along with various combinations of those options. "We're taught from an early age that there's one linear career path to success, and you go from one step to the next," she says, but this alternative career model instead suggests that there are many different ways to be successful, and each person should define that path for themselves. Part of the new model also involves adapting the mentality that you work for yourself, even when you work for others, Jamie says—a philosophy that applies perfectly to the career-plus-side-gig model.

That lesson is driven home to me, over and over again, every time I sell another planner, write another freelance article, or plan my next speech. My full-time reporting job is still where I spend most of my time and it provides the bulk of my income; it's also where I find much of my satisfaction, especially when I hear from readers who find a story I wrote useful, or when an article takes off on Twitter or Facebook. With the backing of my employer, I can reach far wider audiences than I ever could on my own. Still, the glee I feel over finishing a new planner, or selling one, or giving a well-received speech, provides a different kind of joy: Creating my money planners and giving talks on money depends on me finding my own voice, and my own skills, and figuring out how that best intersects with what people find useful. That, as the career research suggests, is incredibly satisfying.

If I'm having a bad day at work, all I have to do is scroll through my Etsy feedback for an espresso-level pick-me-up: "So helpful! Love how easy it is to use!" Michelle wrote about one of my money planning kits. "So well thought out and makes managing money more fun," said another customer about my money planner. "As a recent graduate school student, I need a little help to get on track. So far, the worksheets are easy to use and include just enough not to be too overwhelming. Thank you!" wrote another. A woman planning on soon becoming a single mom wrote to me after reading my baby planner, asking if I had any specific advice for single expectant moms. (I told her to be sure to find child care she felt comfortable with as soon as possible.) A customer in Barcelona, Spain, wrote to let me know she was excited to sit down with a cup of coffee and study the money planner. "Thank you for your effort, it is totally worth it!" she wrote. Another Michelle, who purchased the personalized version of my one-page planner, wrote me an enthusiastic email: "You are sending me in the right direction and this is greatly appreciated at the perfect time . . . I can't wait to put the ideas into action."

My planners also helped me accomplish my original goal: greater financial security. In the year since first launching Palmer's Planners, my shop received almost 20,000 page views and sold $2,000 worth of planners. Thanks to my freelance and speaking work, I was able to bring my total outside income to over $10,000, exceeding my original goal. Not enough to sustain me or my family without my full-time job, but a significant figure that I could probably increase if I ever needed to.

The other side-giggers that I met along the way continue to give me inspiration. They convinced me that mixing traditional and new economies into a hybrid career is right for me, and that it's probably right for a lot of other people, too. In another ten years, having a side-gig could be as essential a tool for modern workers as knowing how to type, or how to send email. The good news is that it's also a lot more fun.

TOP TAKEAWAYS

* Many side-giggers have no plans to leave their full-time jobs; their goal is to continue to build their side-pursuits alongside their careers.

* Side-giggers who face unexpected job losses are often able to rebuild their financial lives on the strength of their side-gigs.

* Some side-giggers become so successful that they quit their full-time jobs to make more time for their side-businesses.

* Side-giggers get their satisfaction not just from building financial security, but from making a difference in other people's lives.

Epilogue:
The Future of
Side-Gigs

LAUNCHING AN ONLINE SHOP MIGHT FEEL VERY OF-THE-MOMENT, but it's actually quite retro. People have long relied on side-gigs for security amid economic flux. The *Oxford English Dictionary* dates the first published use of the word *moonlighting* to describe "paid work in addition to one's regular employment" back to 1954.

In the 1950s and 1960s, when the workplace was still largely defined by the *Organization Man* mindset, which emphasized loyalty and conformity over individuality, going off on one's own to earn extra income was often framed in a negative light. In fact, most mentions of the term "moonlighting" in the mainstream press described violations of existing rules. In 1969, the *New York Times* reported on potential new conflict-of-interest legislation to prohibit public employees from simultaneously working for private companies. It also wrote about New York policemen who were prohibited from moonlighting at the Woodstock festival after their supervisor ruled it would violate regulations.

That judgmental attitude toward anyone seeking to earn extra money through a side-gig continued into the disco era. In the early 1970s, you were still more likely to read about moonlighting in the crime pages than the career pages. The discomfort with the concept of earning extra money outside a full-time job was palpable; it was demonized like a war enemy or a cheating spouse. It disrupted the natural order of things, and those in power—bosses, newspaper editors—resisted it.

As the decade continued, and moonlighting became more mainstream and even accepted, at least by workers looking for ways to boost their pay, the press focused more on what supervisors could do to crack down on it. *The American Banker* ran a feature on how to stop employees from taking on other jobs in their free time; ideas included offering them recreational programs to keep them busy. Congress passed new laws to prohibit lawmakers (along with other federal officials) from earning more than $15,000 (almost $65,000 in today's dollars) a year through outside work, such as speaking engagements. A New York carpenters' union proposed a new rule prohibiting moonlighting, especially by public employees, presumably because it was taking work away from its members. Federal auditors complained that university professors, who consulted on the side for federal agencies, took on so much outside work for other contractors that they were short-changing the government. In a 1978 article, *Newsweek* described professors moonlighting as consultants as a "growing problem in the nation's colleges."

Pop culture also reflected the belief that working side-jobs could only lead to trouble: On the *Mary Tyler Moore Show*, the character Murray ran into trouble after trying to boost his news-writing income by teaching a night class at a nearby college. The television station prohibited employees from taking on second jobs, and Murray was portrayed as being unable to handle the demands of both.

At the same time, reporters and editors started recognizing the legitimate motivations of many side-giggers: They were just trying to support their families during difficult economic times. A 1979 *Washington Post* feature profiled teachers who felt they had to moonlight to make ends meet, given their relatively low salaries. It found that in one local county, most teachers held second and third jobs. A 1979 story in my own magazine, *U.S. News & World Report*, reported that families were dealing with rising prices by picking up extra jobs on the side. As the article put it, "Working wives, moonlighting and overtime are the order of the day." At the time, none of those situations were considered desirable, even if they were increasingly necessary.

A federal analysis of 1970s jobs data noted that the primary options for families looking to increase their household income were for either the wife to join the workforce or the husband to pick up a second job. Indeed, the decline in husbands holding second jobs in the 1970s was correlated with an uptick in wives holding first jobs. By the end of the decade, about 6.2 percent of husbands, and 5 percent of the general population, held more than one job, and it was usually in response to the desire to earn more money.

The first foreshadowing of the excitement and empowerment that side-gigs can bring came from the *Washington Post* Style section in August 1979. It profiled a forty-two-year-old car salesman moonlighting as a "hair sculptor," a term he used to mean hair styling plus a hint of therapy. As the reporter put it, "you can get the layered look and, at the same time, get in touch with your feelings." The car salesman had taken a standard profession and customized it, which gave him clients, coverage in the local paper, and a steady side income.

That far more positive embrace of side-gig culture continued into the decade that also embraced other rebellions, from Madonna to heavy metal. Throughout the 1980s, newspapers and magazines reported on Americans using side incomes to shore up their precarious financial states. The *Miami Herald* profiled a merchandise manager who started using his career skills to help neighbors organize their garage sales (in exchange for 10 percent of the sales). "Two jobs can work," the headline proclaimed. In 1983, the how-to book by Jay David, *How to Play the Moonlighting Game*, came out, making further converts.

Still, many stories emphasized the hardships associated with managing more than one job, rather than the benefits. A 1989 *Chicago Tribune* story described moonlighting as a means of "survival," especially for single women without the second income of a partner. It profiled one thirty-year-old woman who worked as a New York Stock Exchange sales assistant by day and chef and caterer by night. "It's a grueling pace. . . . But to survive in New York as a single woman, you really have to be a creative economist. Often that means taking a second job," she said. The rest of the article focused on the stress of dividing one's time between two jobs, and even quoted a workplace psychologist on how the situation can leave women exhausted and angry.

At the same time, Bureau of Labor Statistics reports show that the number of people holding multiple jobs was starting to skyrocket and that women were experiencing the biggest surge. The economic growth of the 1980s meant that more jobs were available, and Americans embraced the opportunity to increase their income, especially after the recessions in the earlier part of the decade. Between 1980 and 1989, the number of people moonlighting increased by 52 percent, to a total of 7.2 million people, or 6.2 percent of all workers— the highest rate in over three decades.

As one might expect from the uptick in women joining the workforce at the time, women were responsible for much of that increase. The number of women who held more than one job doubled during the 1980s, to a record level of 5.9 percent by 1989. (Women who were widowed, divorced, or separated had a 7.2 percent rate of moonlighting.) At the end of the decade, 43 percent of moonlighters were women, compared to just 15 percent in 1970, the Bureau of Labor Statistics reports. The people most likely to take up second jobs were the ones in the "crunch" years of juggling family responsibilities, between the ages of thirty-five and forty-four. Affording household expenses was cited as the most common reason for doing so.

Moonlighting was further validated—and its spot in mainstream America confirmed—by *Moonlighting*, a television series on ABC starring Bruce Willis and Cybill Shepherd that aired during the last half of the 1980s. Shepherd's character helped run the detective agency headed by Willis's character after she went bankrupt. Like many of the side-giggers profiled in this book, she leverages her connections as a former model to make the new business a success.

Then, in the 1990s, the acceptance and even glamorization of a multi-income lifestyle really came into its own: Instead of hit men and criminals, moonlighting now belonged to the rich and powerful. In one of the first uses of the term "side-gig" in the mainstream press, a 1990 feature in the *Chicago Tribune* described Scott Turow's career as a bestselling novelist as a "side-gig" that accompanied his legal career. In 1999, the publication *Chief Executive* described a health care executive's role on another company's board as a "side-gig."

Meanwhile, the Bureau of Labor Statistics reported that highly educated, highly paid workers were also among those most likely to pick up second jobs, partly because they tended to have more flexibility with their schedules, along with skills that allowed them to generate significant income from those outside pursuits. The rate of multiple job holding continued to hover at 6.3 percent for all workers, with the most educated jobholders—those holding master's degrees or PhDs—boasting rates of over 9 percent. The most common reasons included meeting household expenses, paying off debt, pure enjoyment, shoring up savings, and wanting to build a business. Moonlighting was increasingly a sign of success, rather than desperation.

Around the same time, career advice columnists started actively urging readers to pursue side-gigs. In stark contrast to the 1978 *Newsweek* article on university professors shortchanging their federal contracts because of too much moonlighting, a 1996 story in *Black Issues in Higher Education* celebrated professors who pick up side-gigs: "Moonlighting becomes them," the story declared, before going on to point out that professors use their side-gigs to not only boost their income but also to get ahead in the academic world. Similarly, a headline in a 1994 *Computer World* confirmed, "Moonlighting gets respectable." A 1997 *Florida Times-Union* article asked, "Computer programmers do it. So do carpenters, tree surgeons and mechanics. Accountants, too. What they're doing is moonlighting. So why not you?" That same year, syndicated Knight-Ridder career columnist Amy Lindgren dished out tips on how to find second jobs and how to handle the additional pressures of moonlighting. A 1999 *Ebony* story headlined "Success Secrets of Young Entrepreneurs" emphasized the benefits of launching a business while still employed full time elsewhere.

Self-described serial moonlighter Roger Woodson shared his advice in his 1997 book *Modern Moonlighting: How to Earn Thousands Extra Without Leaving Your Day Job*. "There was a time when working a second job made a person look or feel inadequate as a provider. This is no longer the case. Today's modern moonlighters are turning their time off into hefty bank accounts, new careers, and new businesses. There is no shame in working for yourself after the whistle blows on your day job," he wrote. After working as a plumber for a company by day and taking on extra plumbing jobs at night, Woodson also built a series of other side-gigs: teaching plumbing, serving as a wedding photographer, writing, and breeding dogs. While the thrust of his argument still resonates, his advice for readers also shows how much has changed in the fifteen years since he wrote his book: He focuses on mail-order businesses instead of the world of online sales, and in-person, labor-intensive gigs such as providing diaper-cleaning services or selling secondhand clothes instead of creative services, the far more popular choice today.

Throughout the 2000s, we again saw some backlash, particularly from companies worried that their side-gigging employees were shortchanging their full-time work. "Don't allow moonlighting by workers to erode profits," warned a 2001 article in a trade publication for contractors. In 2003, *Washington Post* career columnist, Mary Ellen Slayter, reminded readers that even moonlighters need to remember that "job one is job one." In 2006, another trade publication declared, "Let's put an end to moonlighting." That pushback shows just how firmly the concept of earning income from multiple sources had entrenched itself into our culture and had become a way of life for many Americans.

Today, many new college grads assume that they will build a side-gig in addition to whatever full-time job they are able to land. The 2011 Youth Entrepreneurship Study by Buzz Marketing Group and the Young Entrepreneur Council found that 36 percent of respondents, who were between the ages of sixteen and thirty-nine, had started side-businesses in order to bring in more income. Those businesses included freelance work, eBay shops, tutoring, baking, and web design.

That helps explain why today, side-gig culture is blowing up. Federal statistics show that the high rates for moonlighting that we first saw in the 1990s continue, particularly among those with advanced degrees, and surveys that pick up smaller-level freelance and contract work, such as the MetLife survey quoted in the Introduction, suggest far higher rates of side-gigging.

For many of the side-giggers who invited me into their homes and lives, running a side-gig felt like the obvious choice, just as getting a nine-to-five job for life might have to our grandfathers. Twenty-somethings in particular often responded to my questions about why they had side-gigs as if I asked them why they had a Facebook account. Why wouldn't they?

The belief that everyone needs a Plan B shows up even in places where you might not expect career advice. On a recent cab drive, the friendly driver asked me about my line of work, and then asked, "What would you do if you got laid off?" Many of his cab driver friends, he explained, were trained as doctors and engineers in their home countries, and, unable to find employment in their professions in the United States, became cab drivers. Everyone, he told me, needs a similar backup plan.

The rapper Slim Thug makes the same point in his 2012 personal finance e-book, *How to Survive in a Recession*, which was written primarily for aspiring hip-hop artists. "One hustle is never enough," he writes. "If you're working at 7-11, have some other hustle when you're not working. Your side hustle could be anything—selling DVDs, a sports fantasy thing, or whatever you are into. You don't want to put all your eggs in one basket."

That hearty embrace of side-gigs from so many sources makes it easy to imagine a day when side-gigs are even more widespread than they are today, as ubiquitous as smartphones or email addresses. Instead of focusing so heavily on corporate recruiting and job openings, forward-thinking college career offices will emphasize how students can build marketable skills on their own, through entrepreneurial projects. New college graduates will expect to pair more traditional office jobs with after-hours freelance work. The back-and-forth seesaw between full-time employment and side-gig might sway more heavily in one direction during different stages of life: Young entrants into the workforce might expect to pick up side-gigs in order to supplement relatively low incomes, gain experience, and support themselves if they're unable to find full-time work.

After having children, parents might scale back full-time jobs and make up for lower salaries with the more flexible work of a side-gig. And retirees might ramp up side businesses to supplement savings and to stay active and relevant in their fields, especially if they were forced to retire early.

As a result, we'll probably see more double-sided business cards featuring full-time jobs on one side and side-gigs on the back, social media accounts that list primary jobs alongside freelance offerings, and personal websites that seamlessly blend those dual identities. Workers will demand more flexible schedules—and corporate rules— to provide time for their side-careers, and companies will likely acquiesce because they know that flexibility benefits them, too, by allowing them to hold onto their top employees while they gain extra skills. More detailed workplace policies will allow for that elasticity while minimizing conflicts of interest.

We can also expect to see more organizations, associations, Facebook pages, and Meetup groups dedicated to supporting side-giggers with camaraderie, marketing assistance, and brainstorming help. Home office nooks to allow for brief spurts of work, on weekends and in the evenings, will be even more popular than they already are, along with apps and planners that allow people to juggle their multiple roles. The Bureau of Labor Statistics will likely finesse its methods of collecting information on multiple job holders to more fully capture the side-gigging segment of the population, as former Office of Management and Budget director Peter Orszag recently urged. Most importantly, perhaps, any stigma or embarrassment that currently comes from acknowledging a side-gig will disappear, as politicians and economists recognize that side-giggers are an increasingly vital and powerful part of our economy—not just our personal economies.

When I checked back in with side-giggers months after first interviewing them, as I was completing this book, their updates underscored their continuous flexibility and willingness to adapt to both economic conditions and their own life circumstances. Here are their stories:

► **Chris Furin,** the cake baker profiled in Chapter 1, has expanded significantly since I first visited his home kitchen in the fall of 2011. His cake business grew so much that he had to move it into a commercial bakery in Kensington, Maryland. He also started selling cookies and cupcakes along with his custom-made cakes. "Between my website, referrals, and positive online reviews, it's enough to keep my phone ringing and emails full of requests. Sometimes I can't even keep up with demand," he says. He hired a part-time worker to help him, and bought a refrigerated van to make deliveries easier. He credits his success to the fact that he launched his business in a field that he already knew well from his years working in his father's deli, as well as to his wife, Dawn, who lent her own marketing expertise to help him build up his web presence.

► **Nicole Crimaldi Emerick**, the founder of MsCareerGirl.com, also featured in Chapter 1, launched a second company, MCG Media, which offers online marketing services to companies. While Nicole initially embraced her new identity as a full-time entrepreneur after she was unexpectedly laid off from a start-up, she ultimately decided that she preferred the financial stability of having a full-time job while keeping her own entrepreneurial pursuits as a side-gig. "It's been really tough, but this year has also taught me a lot about financial management, what being self-employed is really like, and to appreciate all of the resources that bigger companies have," she says. She recently landed a new full-time job as a senior social strategist at a digital agency in Chicago. As the agency's first and only social media specialist, she now draws heavily on her experiences as the founder of her two companies to create social media campaigns for brands. "Had I not been self-employed first, I'm not sure I'd be able to keep up with the demands of my new role," she says.

► **Amy Stringer-Mowat**, the Etsy seller in Chapter 2 who inspired me to open my own shop, continues to grow her cutting board shop, while also juggling being the mother to a toddler. Her sales have doubled in the last year, and she and her husband launched their own website, www.aheirloom.com, to complement their Etsy shop. The shop was recently featured in *Time* magazine and they have several new products in the works, too.

► **Emily Beach**, the hockey coach and training stick inventor from Chapters 2 and 3, continues to collect orders for her Dribble Dr. sticks and will soon start showcasing an indoor version. She's so busy with her full-time job coaching hockey that she's always looking for ways to find more time to build her business at the same time.

► **Megan Moynihan Callaway**, the public relations freelancer from Chapter 4, has settled into her dream life: She spends the winter months in Jackson Hole, Wyoming, where she and her husband ski, and then the rest of the year in New York City. She's built up her client base to four steady clients, including an Irish baby products company, and named her company Callaway Communications. "I'm reaching my capacity and readjusting to having a pretty full workload, so if I take on any new clients, they'll have to be smaller in size and I'll likely charge higher rates," she says. For now, she'd rather stay small than hire employees or collaborate with other freelancers. Her manageable client load lets her live the lifestyle she wants: She and her husband are planning a three-week trip to Hawaii after they wrap up the ski season in Jackson Hole. "We'll work shorter days, from 8 a.m. to noon, and then surf in the afternoon," she says.

► **Emily Miethner**, the founder of NY Creative Interns also in Chapter 4, first reduced her hours to part time at her day job working as community manager for the website RecordSetter.com so she could focus more on building NY Creative Interns, and then she decided to leave altogether. "We just celebrated our two-year anniversary [at NY Creative Interns] and got a lot more people to come to events and more people wanting to work with us, so I felt like now was the time to take advantage of that," she says. While she doesn't yet pay herself out of her NY Creative Interns work, she supports herself by taking on related freelance gigs—she speaks at colleges, gives workshops on social media and career management, and works with a nonprofit on internships.

► DesignedGood cofounder **Katy Gathright**, who was profiled in Chapter 5, has moved full steam ahead with the website's launch. The company has since sold direct trade chocolate, infinity scarves, and fair trade soccer balls to their members, among other ethically appealing items. She and her cofounders are busy lining up more brands, attending industry conferences, and spreading the word about their company.

► Chapter 5's **Peter Davis**, the college student and founder of community-building website CommonPlace, has also enjoyed rapid expansion. CommonPlace is now in twenty towns, with plans to be in every town in Massachusetts by the end of 2013. He and his team have also built revenue streams through the local "marketplace" aspect of the sites, where neighbors can find furniture, coupons, services, and tickets to events. "If we take a percentage cut from all the exchanges we facilitate, we'll be able to do a lot of things at once: Provide a revenue stream, avoid banner ads, and support local businesses and service providers," he says. His team is also looking into potential relationships with larger organizations, such as newspaper chains and groups such as Rotary and Boy Scouts.

► Professional opera singer **Jessi Baden-Campbell**, profiled in Chapter 6, left her meeting planner position for a new full-time job as a coordinating producer at a production company. She still sings as a church soloist every Sunday and performs at her children's school, but has scaled back her singing work because of the demands of her new job. Still, she makes use of her downtime to practice. Instead of lunchtime concerts in the parking garage, she rehearses during her forty-minute commute.

► As Chapter 6's **Corinne Delaney** worked on updating her website and finding new clients, her alma mater, James Madison University, asked her to sing the National Anthem at the homecoming game in the fall of 2012. Standing in front of about 25,000 people in a bright red coat, surrounded by the school's marching band, she sang as her face and name were broadcast on the stadium's Jumbotron. "It was an amazing experience," says Corinne. She continues to pick up more gigs for smaller events, as well.

► Juppy inventor **Jeffrey Nash**, also profiled in Chapter 6, says that while revenue has not yet reached the $250,000 a year he anticipated, his company is still bringing in enough to fund his retirement, which is more than he could ever say about his former Men's Wearhouse job. He's also working on improving the Juppy model itself, as well as deals with other companies that could help increase sales.

► Chapter 6's **Ebony Utley**, the professor, writer, and speaker, enjoyed her sabbatical so much that she says she wishes it lasted forever. She promoted her first book, *Rap and Religion*, while also conducting the research for her next book, *Shades of Infidelity*. She hasn't picked up as many paid speaking engagements as she would like, which she attributes to the economy, but she continues to build her reputation as a go-to expert on race and communication.

► **Ben Popken,** the journalist and improv comic from Chapter 7 who experienced a layoff, landed a new full-time job as a senior staff writer and editor at NBCNews.com. He also became a dad, and decided to stop performing improv. "I did enjoy improv, but I'm not sure if I'll go back. . . . Improv is so ephemeral, and in some ways it seems silly to spend so much time on something that evaporates when it's over." With the demands of fatherhood and a full-time office job, he says that if he does find time to work on comedy, it will be comedy writing, or videos. For Ben, the shift from freelancer to staffer is a welcome one: "Knowing that I have a steady stream of income to rely on, and a secure position, helps relieve some anxieties and lets us make plans for the future more boldly," he says.

► **Jason Nicholas**, the veterinarian from Chapter 8 who was raising money through IndieGoGo to publish his cat and dog safety books, reached his goal. He raised just over $15,000, which has allowed him to finalize publication of his dog safety book as well as market it. He recently sent it off to the printer, and he's already had a few bulk preorders. After he's promoted the dog book, he'll finish the cat safety one.

▶ **Jeff Frederick,** the architect in Chapter 9 who built his freelance business through Elance.com to get him through unemployment patches, continues to run a brisk freelance business on the side. One Elance client brought him out to Nebraska to see the finished products based on his designs and to explore a new project in the same building. Connections that he made through Elance also led to new work near his home in Michigan. "Working full time and moonlighting can be time-consuming and stressful, but also rewarding. I've found that if I'm honest with my clients and tell them that I mainly work nights and weekends on their projects, they are quite understanding," he says.

My own life has also changed since I first started my side-gig. Just over a year after opening up my Etsy shop, we welcomed our new baby son, Neal, into the world. Becoming a family of four intensified my desire to earn extra money while also making it more difficult to do so. As I took care of Neal during my maternity leave from my full-time job, I continued selling planners, sending them to customers while he napped. As he gets bigger and more self-sufficient, I plan to keep growing my shop and, I hope, my income.

Side-giggers are able to continually knock down and recreate game plans like Legos. Different skills, passions, and pursuits can be mixed and matched, like colorful building blocks, to create new revenue streams when another comes crashing down. And as a result of that flexibility, life can feel a little more stable—even in an economy that isn't.

The Economy of You
Handbook

EXERCISES AND WORKSHEETS

EVEN AFTER YOU'VE COMMITTED TO STARTING A SIDE-GIG, DOING SO can be overwhelming. Where do you start? What should you do? How do you find the time?

This section functions as your own side-gig starter kit: It is designed to help you generate ideas, get ready to launch, and hone your plans.

If you're still on the fence about launching a venture at all, then the questions in "Are You Ready to Launch Your Side-Gig?" will help you decide if now is the time to go for it. If you're not sure what type of side-gig makes the most sense for you, the "Find Your Gig" worksheet will help point you in the right direction. And the worksheets on your game plan, pitches, and money will keep you on track as you map out your own path to increased financial security. You can also download illustrated versions at economyofyou.com.

The handbook includes:

- ► Are You Ready to Launch Your Side-Gig?

- ► Find Your Gig

- ► Create a Game Plan

- ► Pitching Worksheet and Pitch Tracker

- ► Make Your Money Work

ARE YOU READY TO LAUNCH YOUR SIDE-GIG?

These simple yes/no questions will help you gauge your readiness to get started on a new, and potentially lucrative, adventure.

1. Do you worry about losing your job?

2. Do you wish you could earn more money?

3. Is your full-time job and personal life stable enough that you can dedicate at least one to two hours a week to a new pursuit?

4. Do you have a hobby that could turn into a profit-making enterprise?

5. Do people come to you for advice or guidance on something you're good at?

6. Do you have a skill that you use in your day job that is valuable to other people?

7. Do you enjoy marketing yourself and reaching out to people online?

8. Has your income in your day job stagnated?

9. Are you ready to invest in yourself and try out a new identity as an entrepreneur?

10. Do you believe that you have something useful to offer the world that you haven't yet explored?

If you answered "yes" to most of these questions, congratulations: You are side-gig ready. Use the "Find Your Gig" tool below to help zero in on your ideal pursuit.

FIND YOUR GIG

Want a side-gig but aren't sure where to start? This worksheet will help you sort through your six primary options, which revolve around creating products, providing a service, running a business, helping others, doing physical work, and performing.

Create: Do you have any creative passions or hobbies? List them here.

1. _____
2. _____
3. _____

Can you imagine selling creations based on those hobbies, either online or in-person?

If you enjoy blogging, cooking, inventing, writing, or a myriad of other creative pursuits, then you can probably find a way to make money from them, too. With the growth of websites such as Etsy.com and Amazon Marketplace, it's easier than ever to sell your creations online, and to find buyers through social media. Creating is one of the most common ways to earn money on the side; examples include the husband-and-wife team who invented the "Can I Buy?" app (Chapter 2), hockey training stick inventor Emily Beach (Chapters 2 and 3), and children's book author Calee Lee (Chapter 3). Related side-gigs on the Top Fifty list include baker (#12), fine artist (#27), and florist (#32).

Service: Do you have skills that you've built up over time, perhaps through your full-time job, that are hard to attain and valuable to others? List them here.

1. _____
2. _____
3. _____

THE ECONOMY OF YOU

Circle the skills listed above that are most valuable to other people.

This category contains a wide range of skilled work, and is also the most likely to involve side-gigs that require some kind of licensing or specific training. (To avoid breaking any laws, first check to see if your local or state government has any requirements.) Examples include legal services, financial services, marketing, security, information technology services, beauty treatments, and massage. Kylie Ofiu (Chapter 2) cuts hair, tax expert Jason Malinak shares his knowledge with customers (Chapter 3), and Lucinda Lyon-Vaiden practices massage and acupuncture (Chapter 6). Top Fifty examples include financial services provider (#3), legal services provider (#4), and makeup artist (#49).

Run: Do you enjoy managing other people, money, and projects? Does the idea of being a small business owner appeal to you? What type of business can you imagine running? What would most leverage your current contacts, experience, and resources? Make a list of potential business here.

1. _____
2. _____
3. _____

This category works best for people who like being in charge; they enjoy the independence and challenge that comes from being a small business owner. Often the idea starts from a casual side-gig, perhaps a creativity-fueled or service-oriented one, and then blossoms into a full-blown business. Examples include cake-maker Chris Furin (Chapter 1), jewelry store owner Erica Sara (Chapter 4), and art studio owner Stephanie Theodore (Chapter 6). Almost all of the examples on the Top Fifty list can be turned into full-fledged small businesses.

Help: Do you get energized from spending time with other people? What types of activities with other people are both enjoyable to you and useful to others? List them here.

1. _____
2. _____
3. _____

Circle the ones on your list that you could imagine people paying you for.

If you'd rather spend the day with other people than on your own, then a side-gig that involves working with others is probably for you. Teaching (at a university like Melissa Van Orman in Chapter 6), coaching (as Sydney Owen of Chapter 3 does), or consulting (like Tara Gentile of Chapter 1) are common options. Working one-on-one with clients or students, sharing knowledge or expertise that you have, can be deeply fulfilling. Top Fifty examples include social media consultant (#5), life coach (#18), and education and training consultant (#14).

Do: Do you find physical activity enjoyable and satisfying? List the activities that appeal to you below.

1. _____
2. _____
3. _____

Which of the activities you listed also function as a service people are likely to pay for? Circle those with profit potential.

If you enjoy physical work, opportunities abound, because many people prefer to outsource that work, or at least get help with it. Gardening and dog-walking are two of the most popular options. Tara Heuser of Chapter 2 built a pet-sitting business and Nicholas Ignacio of Chapter 6 started a lawn care services company. Examples from the Top Fifty list include handyman (#22), home organizer (#33), and personal shopper (#35).

Perform: Do you have unique abilities and talents that you enjoy performing for others? Are these unique talents something that people would potentially pay to see you perform? List those unique skills and talents here, and consider who the potential audience might be.

1. _____
2. _____
3. _____

People with unique talents or abilities can often find paying audiences or sponsors. Examples include singers, stand-up comics, professional athletes, and clowns. Jessi Baden-Campbell from Chapter 6 sings opera and Alisha Williams (also Chapter 6) runs. Related side-gigs on the Top Fifty list include keynote speaker (#20), comedian (#43), and disc jockey (#31).

CREATE A GAME PLAN

This checklist takes you through the steps to turn a side-gig idea into a steady source of income.

1. *Explore what motivates you most.*

❑ Why do you want your side-gig to succeed?

❑ Have you recently experienced a major life change?

❑ Do you feel financially stressed?

2. *Pick the side-gig that's best suited to your background, life-style, and personality.*

❑ Browse the Top Fifty Side-Gigs list, as well as sites that list the products and services of other side-giggers (such as Etsy.com, Freelancer.com, and Craigslist.org), to see what most appeals to you.

❑ Use the "Find Your Gig" tool above.

❑ Experiment with your selected gig by putting your product or service out into the world, via blog, Twitter, or an established website (such as Etsy.com, Fiverr.com, or Freelancer.com) and see if you have any buyers.

❑ Take another small step, such as launching a blog, related to your side-gig idea.

3. *Get on top of your financial life.*

❑ Review your finances, paying special attention to any weak spots. Do you need to focus on scaling back spending or paying off debt? Do you have an emergency savings account with at least three months worth' of expenses?

❑ Use a free online tool such as Mint.com to create a budget and savings goals.

❑ Make a plan to pay off any burdensome debt.

❑ Ramp up savings to give yourself more flexibility and peace of mind. When you start earning money from your side-gig, save that revenue. Track any expenses related to your side-gig carefully for tax purposes.

❑ Fill out the "Make Your Money Work" worksheet on pages 171–172.

4. *Find new friends who are also engaged in similar side-gig pursuits.*

❏ Start reading blogs or web forums related to your side-gig.

❏ Join a Meetup.com group or online group of people who also do similar work.

❏ Create Twitter and other social media accounts to help make those connections. Retweet other people's ideas, reply to their questions, "like" their Facebook pages, and engage in back-and-forth dialogue with the people in your field that you admire.

5. *Promote your side-gig vigorously, by blogging, Tweeting, and other online efforts.*

❏ Give yourself a social media makeover: Dedicate five to ten minutes a day to sending relevant Tweets or other messages via social media.

❏ Check your brand: Run a web search on your name to see what people learn about you online.

❏ On your online profiles on social media accounts, describe yourself in terms of your new side-gig identity to help spread the word about what you're offering.

❏ Make a list of your ideal clients or customers and create targeted pitches for them; the pitching template on page 170 can help.

6. *Create time in your week.*

❏ Organize household maintenance to spend as little time on it as possible; devote those extra hours to your side-gig.

❏ Create a physical space in your home to work on your side-gig, even if it's in a closet or corner.

❏ Wake up a half-hour early (or more) to devote this quiet time to your new pursuit, or take advantage of lunchtime to make progress by sending pitch e-mails, writing blog posts, or sending Tweets.

❏ Implement the organization system that works best for you, whether it's via a day planner, app, or Google calendar. Use it to stay on top of commitments across all aspects of your life, including full-time work, side-gigs, family, and household management.

7. *Find ways to be resilient.*

- ❏ Learn how to cheer yourself up in the face of disappointment.

- ❏ Take care of yourself by eating well, exercising, and getting enough sleep.

- ❏ Draw on your support network, whether it's family or virtual friends online, to get you through down times.

8. *Help others in your community.*

- ❏ Answer emails sent to you asking for advice, even if briefly; be helpful whenever possible.

- ❏ Hire other side-giggers to do work that you can't do yourself, such as web design or marketing.

- ❏ Become a useful source of information through your social media accounts or blog.

9. *Make a long-term plan.*

- ❏ Consider how you want to grow (or not grow) your business, whether it's ultimately selling it to another person or company, staying small, or expanding to include multiple employees. Do you want your side-gig to always be "on the side," or do you want to leave your full-time job and turn it into your main gig?

- ❏ Think about the legacy that you are building with your side-gig, and whether you want to tweak it at all, or add a more explicit charitable component.

PITCHING WORKSHEET

The answers to the questions below will help you pinpoint your audience.

1. Who is my ideal customer? What websites and blogs do they read; where do they shop?

2. What do I have to offer them? How do my products or services help them?

3. Why did I start my business; what motivates me? Is there a story I can share with potential customers?

4. What existing resources, friends, and connections do I have that could help me find that ideal audience?

5. What big websites, blogs, or publications do I dream of being featured in?

Use the Pitch Tracker below to help stay organized

PITCH TRACKER

Pitch List (name)	Follow-up (dates)	Response (Y/N)	Success (Y/N)
_____	_____	_____	_____
_____	_____	_____	_____
_____	_____	_____	_____
_____	_____	_____	_____
_____	_____	_____	_____
_____	_____	_____	_____
_____	_____	_____	_____
_____	_____	_____	_____

MAKE YOUR MONEY WORK

Answer the questions below to help you get on top of your finances.

What are your primary financial goals for the next five to ten years? (Examples: Pay off debt, buy house, save $50,000)

1. _____
2. _____
3. _____
4. _____
5. _____

What does financial security mean to you?

_____
_____
_____

What steps do you need to take to achieve that definition of financial security?

1. _____
2. _____
3. _____

What can you do to be more frugal? Where do you waste the most money?

1. _____
2. _____
3. _____

What's your best money habit that you want to continue?

_____
_____

What will earning extra income from a side-gig allow you to do?

1. _____
2. _____
3. _____

Where do your finances currently stand? In each category below, write down your biggest challenges, goals, and progress:

Savings: _____
_____
_____

Earnings: _____
_____
_____

Debt: _____
_____
_____

Investments: _____
_____
_____

Other: _____
_____
_____

Current net worth: _____
_____
_____

Goal net worth: _____
_____
_____

A

The Top Fifty Side-Gigs

THESE SIDE-GIGS WERE SELECTED AND RANKED BASED ON A MIXTURE of objective and subjective measures. I started by gathering all of the publicly available data from the Bureau of Labor Statistics (BLS) on people who hold more than one job. The BLS puts out useful (and voluminous) information on hundreds of occupations and industries, including how much job holders work and, to some extent, their motivation for doing so. The Bureau's *Occupational Outlook Handbook* similarly contains details on job growth, descriptions, and training requirements across many fields.

Then, I examined reports from other sources, including Freelancer.com, Elance.com, and Payscale.com, all of which have access to the working habits of tens of thousands of people. After creating a raw list of the side-gigs that are the most popular, well-paid, and easiest to launch based on those sources, I used my own interviews with side-giggers and career experts to flesh out the rest.

While the list cuts across many different fields, from agriculture to technology, the focus, as with the rest of this book, is on side-gigs that most appeal to educated, web-savvy professionals looking for additional financial security. The side-gigs featured here tend to have low barriers to entry and high potential for pay. That's why you won't find many minimum-wage paying gigs on this list, but you'll see a preponderance of jobs that can be scaled up and branded with a side-gigger's own unique twist. After all, as this book shows, that's one of the secrets to side-gig success.

THE MASTER LIST

1. Website designer
2. Marketing consultant
3. Financial services provider
4. Legal services provider
5. Social media consultant
6. Fitness trainer
7. Writer
8. Chef
9. Graphic designer
10. Architect
11. App developer
12. Baker
13. Voice actor
14. Education and training consultant
15. Interior designer/decorator
16. Illustrator
17. Landscape designer
18. Life coach
19. Web developer
20. Keynote speaker
21. Gardener
22. Handyman
23. Career coach
24. Tattoo artist
25. Event planner
26. Pet sitter
27. Fine artist
28. Online community builder
29. Software-specific consultant
30. Yoga teacher
31. Disc jockey
32. Florist
33. Home organizer
34. Singer/musician
35. Personal shopper
36. Video editor
37. Babysitter
38. Construction worker
39. Dancer/actor/performer
40. Nutritionist
41. Blogger
42. Data enterer
43. Comedian
44. Copywriting
45. Search engine optimization consultant
46. Information technology consultant
47. Tutor
48. Housekeeper
49. Makeup artist
50. Wedding officiant

1. WEBSITE DESIGNER

Web designers straddle two worlds: the technical and artistic sides of web development. That means they create sites that are both functional and good-looking. Since everyone from large corporations to small-time freelancers need websites these days, their services are in hot demand. That's why website design was listed as one of the fastest growing jobs of 2012 by Freelancer.com, with over 10,000 job listings posted on its site in the first quarter of the year alone. It pays the equivalent of around $60,000 a year, with part-time, freelance graphic web designers pulling in a median rate of almost $30 an hour, according to PayScale.com. For anyone who's already mastered technical and design skills through work experience and experimentation, the start-up costs are minimal—no advanced degrees, formal training, or licenses are required.

BEST FOR: Web and html-savvy designers with free weekend time.

RESOURCES: Freelancer.com, Meetup.com, WebProfessionals.org

Spotlight On ... **Joe DePalma,** art director for a web design company and freelance web designer; age: 32; location: Fairfax, Virginia

Why did you launch your side-business?

JOE D: I have a wife and mortgage and I paid for school myself at Savannah College of Art and Design, which is extremely expensive. That put me in a mountain of debt. With freelancing, I can increase my income by 50 percent. It's not just for the money; I know that eventually, I want to own my own company full time.

How do you avoid conflicts of interest with your full-time job?

JOE D: I don't countermarket against my day job. I don't even have a website that's live right now. All my business is referral-based. There's going to be a conflict of interest if I'm marketing myself against my day job.

How do you find time to do both?

JOE D: I do my freelance work on weekends and evenings. I usually start working again around 8 p.m. and on busy nights I can go until midnight, and then Saturday mornings and Sundays are my busiest times. During the week, I don't always have the energy, especially after cranking it out all day . . . I run out of steam creatively.

What's the hardest part about juggling both your freelance and full-time work?

JOE D: There's only so much time in the day. My day job workweek can be 70 or 80 hours sometimes, and it's draining. Then I go home and I want to spend time with my wife and friends, but it's hard to balance all that out, time-wise and physically.

What's your favorite part about it?

JOE D: I like doing web design, but it's not so much the design part as the service—you're selling your talent and ideas. You take somebody's business and give it structure from a user standpoint. At the end, clients are satisfied and happy because it looks great and functions and they can grow their business because of it.

2. MARKETING CONSULTANT

Marketing consultants help people promote themselves or their products and services. The job includes reaching out to bloggers, social media networks, media contacts, and anyone else who might help get word out about their clients. In addition to working for companies and small businesses, they're often hired by individuals looking for publicity. The median hourly pay for part-time, self-employed marketing consultants is almost $50 an hour, according to PayScale.com, and $59 an hour for the closely related gig of public relations consulting. Start-up costs are low; marketing consultants need the confidence and energy to reach out to new connections, familiarity with social networks such as Twitter and Facebook, and the contacts that come with experience, but no advanced training or degrees are necessary. Still, the time commitment is significant and involves a lot of phone calls, emails, research, and networking.

BEST FOR: Outgoing social media savants who love working with (and helping) other people.

RESOURCES: Elance.com, Meetup.com, American Marketing Association, Internet Marketing Association, copyblogger.com

3. FINANCIAL SERVICES PROVIDER

Side-giggers providing financial services include tax accountants, corporate finance experts, certified financial planners, and a variety of other specialties. Almost all of them require advanced training and licenses, which is why many of them work full time in their field and provide extra services to clients on the side. Pay varies by specialty but tends to be high across the board; PayScale.com reports that the median hourly rate for part-time, self-employed certified financial planners is just over $60 an hour while certified public accountants earn $40 an hour and bookkeepers $19 an hour. Financial services providers tend to take on client-based work, which often means they can set their own schedule and decide how many projects to accept. Start-up costs are medium to high; many financial service providers, including certified financial planners and public accountants, need to be licensed.

BEST FOR: Certified financial professionals with the time, energy, and freedom to take on additional clients.

RESOURCES: National Association of Personal Financial Advisors, Financial Services Institute

> ## Spotlight On ... Joe Cain, certified tax
> specialist and retired New York police officer; age:
> 48; location: New York area

How did you get started?

JOE C: As a foot cop in the Bronx, I knew I needed to buy mutual funds, but I got crushed. I started looking into it and taking tax and finance classes, then started making it a side-gig. I've been preparing taxes for fellow cops since 1989.

What do you like about it?

JOE C: It let me retire. I knew I was leaving, but the side-gig made the decision a no-brainer for me. I loved being a cop, but I was working nonstop. I like numbers and figuring out the tax code and helping people, so decided, this is what I'm going to do.

How do you find clients?

JOE C: They find me through my website, finestfinancial-group.com. I know pensions, I know what they need—80 percent of my clients are cops.

(You can read more about Joe in Chapter 1.)

4. LEGAL SERVICES PROVIDER

Lawyers don't just work in corporate offices; they also take on free-lance projects, which can range from reviewing contracts for fellow side-giggers to consulting work for businesses. Thanks to their high-level training, they command one of the highest hourly rates in side-gig land: PayScale.com reports that part-time, self-employed lawyers earn a median rate of $147 an hour, higher than any other profession. Because most freelance work is project-dependent, side-gig lawyers can often determine their own hours. Start-up costs can be relatively high; in addition to a law degree, many lawyers pick up additional experience by working in specialties in their field and most states require lawyers to update their legal education at least every three years.

BEST FOR: Lawyers with legal interests that extend beyond their day jobs and the time to take on extra work.

RESOURCES: American Bar Association, FreelanceLaw.com, National Association of Freelance Legal Professionals

5. SOCIAL MEDIA CONSULTANT

Social media consultants know Facebook, Twitter, LinkedIn, Pinter-est, and other social networking sites better than anyone else, which is why corporations, small businesses, and even freelancers hire them to help them boost their own outreach efforts. Part-marketing con-sultant (side-gig #2), part-entrepreneur, and part-digital tech guru, social media consulting is growing as fast as the audiences for those networking sites: Twitter- and Facebook-related job postings were among the most popular and fastest growing on Freelancer.com in 2012. According to PayScale.com, part-time, self-employed social media managers earn a median hourly rate of $20 an hour, or the equivalent of around $40,000 a year. The work tends to be client- and project-based, which means it can be scaled up or down as needed. Social media is also a new field; the Bureau of Labor Statistics doesn't yet list it as a distinct profession. Start-up costs are low; social media gurus just need an Internet connection and comfort with social media networks—something many twenty-somethings already have.

BEST FOR: Heavy Twitter and Facebook users who want to put their insider knowledge to good use.

RESOURCES: Mashable.com, ProBlogger.net, AlexisGrant.com, lkrsocialmedia.com, SocialMediaToday.com

6. FITNESS TRAINER

Fitness trainers, who teach everything from weight lifting to aerobics to boxing, tend to be super-fit themselves—after all, their own bodies often serve as their best marketing tool. Many side-gig fitness trainers maintain full-time jobs that are totally unrelated to fitness, which means their side-gig is their chance to embrace their athletic side. Another benefit is that clients often want to meet or take classes after (or before) their own work days or on the weekends, which makes it easier to blend with a typical nine-to-five office job. PayScale.com reports that the median rate for part-time, self-employed fitness trainers, who often lead classes or group sessions, is around $25 an hour. Personal trainers, who usually work one on one with clients, make more; the median hourly rate is $38. Start-up costs are low, although clients and gyms often look for trainers with specialty certifications.

BEST FOR: Outgoing, athletic office workers who want to spend more time at the gym helping other people get fit.

RESOURCES: National Federation of Personal Trainers, Aerobics and Fitness Association of America

7. WRITER

The term "writer" refers to all kinds of ways to use words to make a living, including ghostwriting for another person or corporation, penning technical guides or reports, authoring e-books, and writing freelance magazine articles. In general, the more glamorous it sounds, the less it pays, which is why technical writers are often the best paid of the bunch. (The closely related field of copywriting, side-gig #44, is one of the fastest growing online jobs, but it specifically refers to writing words with the goal of selling products or services.) Part-time, self-employed technical writers earn a median hourly rate of $36, while other types of writers and authors earn around $27 an hour, according to PayScale.com. Related professions include copyediting and proofreading, which generates around $24 an hour. Start-up costs are low to none; writers just need a laptop and Internet connection to get started, and they can often set their own schedules.

BEST FOR: People who love writing as well as promoting their work and marketing themselves online.

RESOURCES: Mediabistro.com, Elance.com, American Society of Journalists and Authors, prowriters.org, Editorial Freelancers Association

8. CHEF

As Food Network watchers know, chefs prepare meals and menus for clients, who can range from restaurant guests to busy families. While anyone can pick up basic cooking skills from watching hours of *Barefoot Contessa* or *Giada at Home*, chefs often undergo extensive training at culinary schools and apprenticeship programs. Two different types of chefs appear on PayScale.com's ranking of the highest paid part-time, freelance workers: executive chefs, who typically work in restaurants or other large-scale kitchens and bring in a median hourly rate of $24.60; and personal chefs, who usually work directly for individual clients and earn $20.10 an hour. The time required is significant; cooking is labor intensive and chefs often work around clients' schedule.

BEST FOR: Advanced home cooks who dream of sharing their talents with the world.

RESOURCES: American Culinary Federation, American Personal and Private Chef Association

9. GRAPHIC DESIGNER

Closely related to both web designers (#1) and illustrators (#16), graphic designers are charged with organizing and presenting concepts on websites or printed material, what colors and styles to use to represent a brand, and communicating complicated ideas in a way that makes sense to readers or viewers. In addition to technical and artistic skills, they also have to know how to work with people, since work tends to be client-based and understanding what a client wants is step number one. Freelance, part-time graphic designers earn a median hourly rate of around $30 an hour, according to PayScale.com. Work tends to be project-based, which means it can be scaled up or down relatively easily. Graphic designers often study art and design in high school or college, but many also teach themselves other aspects of the job, such as how to use the latest design software.

BEST FOR: Artistically gifted and trained designers who enjoy working with others.

RESOURCES: AIGA.org, GraphicArtistsGuild.com

10. ARCHITECT

Wherever you're sitting right now, chances are it's in a space that was designed by an architect. Architects design everything from coffee shops to basement renovations to office buildings. Not surprisingly, they need significant skills and education, including a degree in architecture and state licenses, since they're charged with the safety and soundness of buildings along with aesthetic appeal. That's why many side-gig architects also work in the field full time, supplementing their income with freelance jobs. The Bureau of Labor Statistics expects the field to grow 24 percent between 2010 and 2020, suggesting there is plenty of work available for those with the right credentials. The median hourly pay, according to BLS numbers, is around $36.

BEST FOR: Trained architects who feel underutilized (or underemployed) in their day jobs.

RESOURCES: Elance.com, Guru.com, American Institute of Architects (aia.org).

Spotlight On ... **Jeff Frederick,** freelance and full-time architect; age: 36; location: Troy, Michigan

How did you get started?

JEFF: I'm an architect, and the way the economy was going, especially in Michigan, that meant that a number of the firms I worked with were going through layoffs. My wife is a freelance writer on Elance.com, so when I got laid off, I bid on some jobs there, too, and started getting projects. It helped sustain us through the downtime.

What's your favorite part?

JEFF: The flexibility. I don't have to work from an office, so I can work on it whenever I have time.

Does it help you feel more financially secure?

JEFF: I still needed a full-time job with benefits, but it made a big difference. I'm now back to working full time but I still do Elance projects, because down the road I want to run my own business and choose my own projects.

Does your side-gig work ever conflict with your full-time job?

JEFF: I'm currently an architect for a modular home builder, so there are no conflicts.

(You can read more about Jeff in Chapter 9.)

11. APP DEVELOPER

This job might not have existed a decade ago, but it's a rapidly growing online field today. Freelancer.com ranked it as one of the fastest growing online jobs in 2012. The iPhone app market alone created 4,318 job postings on the site in the first quarter of the year. According to Payscale.com, part-time, self-employed software developers earn a median hourly pay of $40 an hour, which puts them in the top thirty highest-paying part-time, self-employed jobs. App developers can also take a more entrepreneurial route and create apps based on their own ideas, in which case pay depends on the success of those ideas in the marketplace. App development requires significant ease with the ins and outs of programming and technology. That's why many app developers already work in the field of information technology. Because there's so much interest in the growing field, there's also a lot of free information online; Stanford even offers tutorials on app-building through iTunes U.

BEST FOR: Tech gurus who enjoy playing with code in their spare time.

RESOURCES: Freelancer.com, iTunes U

Spotlight On ... **Beena Katekar and Sadhansu Samal,** husband-and-wife team, information technology employees and app developers; ages: 37 and 39, respectively; location: Boston, Massachusetts

Why did you decide to create your own app?

BEENA AND SADHANSU: We didn't see any apps available in the market for what we had in mind (a budgeting app), so we decided to create our own.

What is the hardest part?

BEENA AND SADHANSU: Finding time to discuss concepts with each other and develop them, along with our full-time jobs and two kids.

What's your favorite part of app creation?

BEENA AND SADHANSU: Talking about concepts and getting excited about how each feature of the app will be used, as well as testing the app.

How did you get word out about it?

BEENA AND SADHANSU: We didn't do any marketing whatsoever; sales came from people who were looking for an app and found ours.

(You can read more about Beena and Sadhansu in Chapter 2.)

12. BAKER

Thanks to shows like the Food Network's *Cupcake Wars* and TLC's *DC Cupcakes*, baking has become a side-gig fantasy for many full-time workers. It's also the reality for an increasing number of people, although its popularity exceeds its pay potential. PayScale.com reports that the median hourly pay rate for part-time, self-employed pastry chefs is around $15, which puts it on par with other relatively low-paid fields such as babysitting and house-cleaning. But that doesn't mean it's a bad idea, especially for entrepreneurs who can make their creations stand out against the competition (and therefore can get away with charging customers more). Bakers who create unique brands or focus on specific niches tend to do best. Some bakers also combine their craft with other services or products, such as books, blogging, and workshops. For inspiration, consider the story of Katherine Kallinis and Sophie LaMontagne in Chapter 3, who turned their cupcake business into a reality show (*DC Cupcakes*), two cookbooks (so far), and a thriving online retail shop. Start-up costs can be significant; side-gig bakers can usually work out of their own kitchens (specific license requirements vary by state), but they need ingredients, pans, bowls, and other baking supplies.

BEST FOR: Cupcake-lovers who enjoy dreaming up new concoctions—and who never tire of baking.

RESOURCES: American Pie Council, American Bakers Association, Retail Bakers of America

13. VOICE ACTOR

The demand for voice talent is growing, thanks to the increasing importance of multimedia websites. The freelance website Elance.com singled out voice acting as one of the fastest growing fields in 2012, with a threefold increase in job postings. For those who have the required acting skills, it can be an enjoyable and flexible pursuit, especially with the ease of selling and packaging your voice for online clients through digital technology. For those just getting started, some technical investments might be necessary, including software, microphones, and headsets. Voice acting pay is typically on par with other types of acting, which generates a median hourly rate of around $17.50, according to the Bureau of Labor Statistics.

BEST FOR: Anyone who has ever entertained party guests with impersonations of cartoon characters and celebrities.

RESOURCES: Fiverr.com, Elance.com, VoiceActingAlliance.com, Voice-ActingClub.com

Spotlight On ... **Chris Hardy,** instrument repairman and voice actor, primarily through Fiverr; age: 47; location: Augusta, Georgia

When did you start voice acting?

CHRIS: I watched a lot of cartoons as a kid and was a middle child, and never got the attention that my older and younger siblings got. So I started talking like cartoon characters around the house. Then, when I was twenty-two and ready to get out of the Army, my commander hooked me up with a radio station, and next thing I know, I'm part of a morning show.

What are your most popular orders on Fiverr?

CHRIS: People mostly ask me to speak in a cartoon voice of their choosing, like Homer Simpson's voice.

What's the hardest aspect of it?

CHRIS: When someone orders a big project, like a 3,700-word voiceover. Now I shy away from big projects; I have enough of the small ones.

Do you have advice for other aspiring voice actors?

CHRIS: Treat customers like they're humans. I always try to make it personal and say, "Thanks, Mel, for ordering." Otherwise, I just let the work speak for itself.

14. EDUCATION AND TRAINING CONSULTANT

Education and training consultants typically serve companies and small businesses that need help teaching their employees about everything from how to use new software to how to avoid sexual harassment complaints. The field requires a significant amount of experience and specialization, but it also spans a wide array of fields, from mental health to personal finance, and the Bureau of Labor Statistics reports that almost every industry relies on these types of consultants to some degree. The Bureau reports an increasing demand for this kind of work, too, with the broader category of human resource specialists expected to grow at a brisk 21 percent between 2010 and 2020. For those who already have the skill set, finding gigs is a matter of marketing yourself to potential clients. The potential payoff is high, with PayScale.com reporting that the median hourly rate for self-employed, part-time education and training consultants is just over $56 an hour. Work is intense but project-based, which makes it easy to scale up or down as needed.

BEST FOR: Outgoing types who love public speaking and have valuable skills or expertise to share.

RESOURCES: Society for Human Resource Management

15. INTERIOR DESIGNER/DECORATOR

The fact that an entire cable channel (HGTV) is dedicated to making homes beautiful helps explain the uptick in demand for interior designers and decorators. In fact, the Bureau of Labor Statistics anticipates close to 20 percent growth for the interior design field alone between 2010 and 2020. States often require interior designers to hold licenses, which makes it the ideal side-gig for designers who are already working in the field but want to take on extra, or slightly different, types of work. PayScale.com reports that the median hourly rate for part-time, self-employed interior designers is around $58; for the less technical field of interior decorating, it's $31. Designers with in-demand specialties, such as environmentally friendly design, can often charge more. For those who already hold the necessary degrees and licenses, getting started is just a matter of finding clients.

BEST FOR: Trained designers and decorators who want to explore new projects outside their full-time job.

RESOURCES: HGTV, apartmenttherapy.com, American Society of Interior Designers, DesignSponge.com

16. ILLUSTRATOR

Illustrators are artists who create everything from blog logos to e-book covers to website banners, either by hand or with the assistance of a computer program. Freelancer.com ranked the gig as one of the fastest growing in 2012, with roughly 2,000 new job postings per quarter. Clients range from large companies to freelancers who want to make their blog or website look professional. According to PayScale.com, part-time, self-employed illustrators earn a median hourly rate of $28.40, similar to side-giggers in other creative fields such as graphic design and writing.

BEST FOR: Gifted artists who enjoy working on their own and with clients and who are willing to market themselves and their talents.

RESOURCES: Society of Illustrators, kerismith.com, Etsy.com, dribbble.com (note the three b's), minted.com, cgtextures.com

Spotlight On ... **Lisa Nelson,** illustrator
and Etsy-shop owner; age: 29; location: Holland,
Michigan

How did you get started?

LISA: I was at a job that had all of the Adobe software. I started tinkering around on my breaks, and fell in love. I can't stop doodling flowers now.

Is it hard to find clients?

LISA: Yes and no. It's feast or famine with me. Some weeks I sit there thinking maybe I need to wear a T-shirt that says, "Hire me." Other days, clients come on their own for no apparent reason.

What's your favorite thing about it?

LISA: I love that my job is so flexible. I have a one-year-old and so sometimes I'm not able to work when I want to. This job gives me the ability to be the mom I want to be and also the type of creative that I want to be.

What's the hardest thing?

LISA: The unknown, and not knowing where your next dollar is going to come in. The feeling that I am always "on." I'm always answering emails, or changing diapers, or illustrating new things. It never ends.

How do you manage your time?

LISA: Luckily my daughter still naps twice a day so that frees up a lot of the time for me to do some work. I also take her to daycare twice a week. I think it's healthy and fun for her, and [it's] a way that I can feel like I have had time to dedicate to my work.

Do you have any advice for aspiring illustrators?

LISA: Find your own style. Stick to it. Same goes for routines. Once you find a rhythm with illustrating and living the rest of your life, sink into that. Also, love others . . . Beauty within is revealed in our art.

NOTE: Lisa is the illustrator who designed the Palmer's Planners covers mentioned in Chapter 3.)

17. LANDSCAPE DESIGNER

Landscape design is the outdoor version of side-gig #15, interior designer/decorator. It involves making outdoor space beautiful, usable, and efficient. Clients can range from individuals who are trying to spruce up a backyard to companies with significant green space or local governments with parks and playgrounds. On freelance site Elance.com, landscape design was one of the fastest growing categories for postings in 2012. PayScale.com reports that the median hourly rate for part-time, self-employed landscape designers is close to $26, the equivalent of a $52,000 annual salary.

BEST FOR: Licensed landscape designers itching to pick up new clients and projects, or full-time employees of landscape design firms who want to transition toward self-employment.

RESOURCES: Elance.com, American Society of Landscape Architects

18. LIFE COACH

Life coaching is a rapidly growing, and largely unregulated, field. In fact, the field is so new that the Bureau of Labor Statistics doesn't yet include it on its list of occupations. While several life coaching organizations exist and offer various certification programs, anyone can call themselves a life coach. While that might be considered a good thing to those just entering the field, it also means it can be harder to stand out and distinguish oneself to potential clients. Life coaches usually work one on one with their clients in a mentoring role, encouraging them to define and pursue their goals. Closely related to the fields of therapy and career coaching, life coaches tend to take a more holistic approach, focusing on clients' health and finances as well as life goals. The potential pay is high: PayScale.com ranks life coaches in the top ten–earning part-time, freelance jobs. On average, life coaches bring in a median hourly rate of $70, similar to an information technology consultant. Related professions include more specific coaching fields, such as dating coach or career coach (#23). Since clients often prefer to talk at night or on the weekends, life coaching can mix well with a standard nine-to-five job.

BEST FOR: People with a natural tendency to want to help others with their goals and engage in lengthy conversations about others' lives.

RESOURCES: FindYourCoach.com, the International Coach Federation, the International Association of Coaching, the Spencer Institute, The Coaches Training Institute, CoachInc.com

19. WEB DEVELOPER

In contrast to web designers, web developers focus more on the technical side of websites, although their work often encompasses design aspects, as well. They are also responsible for websites' speed, performance, traffic capacity, and any applications and programs added to the site. As a result of their technical skills, they tend to charge slightly more per hour than web designers: Payscale.com estimates that part-time, self-employed web developers earn around $32 an hour, or about $3 more an hour than web graphic designers. The Bureau of Labor Statistics also lists the field among the fastest growing, with 22 percent growth projected between 2010 and 2020. Start-up costs are minimal, although some web developers opt to earn certifications in specific programs or languages, such as Javascript or html.

BEST FOR: Skilled web developers with full-time jobs who want to expand their client base during off hours, with the possible goal of eventual self-employment.

RESOURCES: Elance.com, webdeveloper.com, International Webmasters Association, WebProfessionals.org

20. KEYNOTE SPEAKER

Getting paid to speak requires comfort in front of large audiences and a platform (such as being known to have some kind of expertise) that leads to speaking invitations. Keynote speakers cover all kinds of topics: overcoming hardship, finding business success, and improving productivity are among the most popular topics at conferences and corporate events. In general, the more well known the speaker, the more they are paid. Fees can range from $500 for small college workshops to $50,000 for talks by big-name celebrities. Keynote speakers are almost always side-giggers; their full-time career and expertise, whether it's in rock-climbing or nonprofit management, is often what gives them the opportunity to get paid to speak. Beyond developing the expertise that leads to speaking engagements, there are few start-up costs for speakers. The biggest challenge is often finding paying clients; many speakers start out speaking for free. The time commitment is significant; each engagement might be just a couple hours long, but speakers typically spend many more hours preparing and perfecting their remarks in addition to traveling.

BEST FOR: Leaders in their fields who enjoy being in the spotlight.

RESOURCES: Toastmasters International, local speakers' bureaus, National Speakers Association

21. GARDENER

Part-time gardeners typically grow flowers or vegetables in their back-yards or in community gardens and sell them to local farmers' markets, specialty stores, or flower shops. While interest in gardening, particularly urban gardening and shared community gardens, has blossomed over the last decade, it's long been a popular side-pursuit: A Bureau of Labor Statistics report on multiple job-holders in 1995 used the term "weekend gardeners" to describe people who "enjoy growing and selling the produce from their small plot." It found the pursuit to be among the most popular types of second jobs. Start-up costs are low; gardeners need access to a plot of land, whether it's at their home or in a shared garden, along with tools and seeds or seed-lings. The time commitment varies by season; during growing season, gardeners can spend much of their weekends and evenings planting, weeding, and harvesting.

BEST FOR: Green thumbs who enjoy spending their free time outdoors and in the garden.

RESOURCES: John Tolluck's The New American Homestead blog (johntullock.blogspot.com), American Community Gardening Association, GardeningMatters.org

22. HANDYMAN

The term "handyman" covers all kinds of odd-job work, from fixing a clogged drain to installing insulation. Busy people are often happy to outsource these kinds of time-consuming jobs to someone who can do it more quickly and efficiently. Licensing requirements vary by state. While handymen increasingly use the Internet to find new clients, word-of-mouth is still the most common marketing method. According to PayScale.com, part-time, self-employed handymen earn a median hourly rate of $24.50, similar to a yoga teacher or executive chef, and pay varies by location. Handymen with advanced expertise in carpentry or other specializations can charge more for their services. Handymen can take on as many or as few jobs when they want, and since many clients want work completed on the weekends, part-time handymen can often combine their work with full-time jobs.

BEST FOR: Men and women who already have home repair skills and who enjoy working with other people in their homes.

RESOURCES: AsktheHandyman.net, Association of Certified Handyman Professionals, HandyAmerican.com, Sidegig.com, Handyman Association of America, United Handyman Association

---

Spotlight On ... James Logie, freelance handyman (while job-hunting for full-time position in environmental mapping); age: 49; location: Silver Spring, Maryland

---

How did you learn to be a handyman?

JAMES: I worked at a nonprofit that renovated inner-city houses and learned on the job.

Does it give you financial security?

JAMES: It's currently my lifeline. I am surviving, but not more than that—I'm not getting ahead. I haven't been able to find a full-time job [since earning a bachelor's degree three years ago]. I'm qualified for an entry-level position in geography or geographic information systems, and there aren't many out there.

How do you find your clients?

JAMES: Through friends and word of mouth. It would take me a while to stop if I did get a full-time job, because people keep asking me to do jobs.

What do you like about it?

JAMES: I like the creativity and thinking through problems to get a solution. I also like that I can take or leave jobs and set my own schedule. That lets me do other creative things, like performing guitar in a waltz band. Doing [handyman work] lets me make those decisions for myself. The trade-off is the paycheck. People's willingness to pay has gone down with the economy; I had to lower my rates to stay employed. In the mid-2000s, I could charge $50 an hour; now I charge closer to $30 an hour.

23. CAREER COACH

Like life coaches, career coaches work one on one with clients to help improve their lives and reach their goals, but with a focus on work. They help people figure out what they most enjoy doing, what their skills are, and how they can move into employment that maximizes their skills and passions. They also help with more specific tasks, such as improving clients' resumes and cover letters. In contrast to certified counselors or therapists, they focus less on emotional history or underlying psychology than the more immediate task of helping clients find satisfying employment. In fact, many career coaches launch their side-businesses without any particular certification or training, but the growth in the industry also means there are many online certification programs available. Certification is optional; earning potential varies by specialization and experience, and is $100 to $500 an hour and up. Scheduling is often flexible and client meetings can take place on weekends and evenings.

BEST FOR: Anyone with a natural tendency to dish out career tips to friends.

RESOURCES: Brazen Careerist, Career Coach Institute, Professional Association of Resume Writers & Career Coaches

Spotlight On . . . **Sydney Owen,** full-time skydiving event coordinator and part-time career coach; age: 28; location: Southern California

How did you get started as a career coach?

SYDNEY: I reviewed a bunch of my peers' resumes in my first couple years out of college. Since I had gotten a job so quickly, they seemed to trust that I knew what needed to happen to make the resume clean and impressive. After a while, it got to the point where I realized this was a service I could offer to young professionals.

What drew you to the field?

SYDNEY: There are so many garbage resumes and so many ridiculously qualified and eager candidates. A bad resume shouldn't prevent a talented individual from getting a great job, but you don't know what you don't know. There is a serious information gap when it comes to what companies are looking for and what we're taught in college when it comes to resumes.

Did you get any special training or certification before launching your coaching business?

SYDNEY: I didn't get any formal training, per se, but I worked with Penelope Trunk, a very well-respected and highly established career coach and author, on my resume when I was still in college. I took what I learned from that experience and built on it.

How do you find clients?

SYDNEY: Currently, it's all word of mouth. I had one girl who gushed about how quickly she got a job after working through her resume with me, and soon enough, I had another client, and then two more clients, and it just kind of rolled from there.

What are your favorite and least favorite parts of coaching?

SYDNEY: My favorite part is when clients get it, when they have the light bulb moment and they're on board with everything they're learning. My process involves them writing the edits themselves, with my guidance, so next time they don't have to hire someone. My least favorite part is finding time to make it work. I work full time as the event coordinator for a skydiving center, so I'm usually pretty beat after a long day of work or jumping, and being on the West Coast, it can be tricky to coordinate times that aren't outrageous for my East Coast clients.

(You can read more about Sydney in Chapter 3.)

24. TATTOO ARTIST

Tattoo artists tend to be highly specialized fine artists—after all, their work is permanently etched on clients' skin, so there's not much room for error. That's why tattoo artists often train, or apprentice, with more experienced artists for years before taking on their own clients. There are also health and hygiene issues to consider, which is why states regulate body art and require various types of coursework, examinations, and licenses. Still, the payoff can be worth the hassle; PayScale.com reports that part-time, self-employed tattoo artists earn a median hourly wage of almost $36, similar to personal trainers and technical writers.

BEST FOR: Artists with an attraction to tattoo culture.

RESOURCES: TattooRoadTrip.com, Tattoo Artists Guild

Spotlight On . . . Pete Dutro, full-time student studying business management and part-time tattooer; age: 37; location: Brooklyn, New York

How did you get started with tattooing?

PETE: I was one of those graffiti kids when I was young, and was really into punk rock and skateboards. I was getting a lot of tattoos, and then I just figured, I should tattoo as well. Now I've been tattooing for about thirteen years.

After you graduate from your business management program, will you continue to work as a tattoo artist?

PETE: I'll always be a tattooer. It's my base profession—if all else fails, I can always tattoo.

How much do you charge?

PETE: It depends on how good you are, but I usually charge around $200 an hour.

How do you find clients?

PETE: Word-of-mouth, mostly. I've been doing it a long time, so a lot of people know of me, and clients know where to find me.

25. EVENT PLANNER

Event planners revel in the details—even when they're for someone else's convention, wedding, or party. Part of the job includes mapping out agendas or schedules, inviting guests, arranging necessary logistics (such as transportation), and handling fees and expenses, including for any contractors involved. The Bureau of Labor Statistics reports rapid job growth in the field, with a projected 44 percent increase in the number of jobs between 2010 and 2020, as organizations look for more ways to connect face to face in a digital age. The median hourly rate for self-employed, part-time event planners is $20, but those with more experience and specialization tend to earn more. The time commitment is big; when an event is approaching, planners often find themselves knee-deep in last-minute requests and questions from clients, attendees, and contractors. Certification programs are available and can make planners more attractive to clients, but they aren't required.

BEST FOR: Anyone with a predilection for details, organization, and parties.

RESOURCES: Convention Industry Council, Society of Government Meeting Professionals, Event Planners Association, Meeting Professionals International, Professional Convention Management Association

26. PET SITTER

Taking care of other people's pets involves everything from walking dogs to spending the night with cats to feeding fish. While it's not very highly paid—PayScale.com puts the going rate for part-time dog walkers at just over $10 an hour—it's a relatively easy gig, particularly for people looking for flexibility. Largely because pet ownership continues to grow, and owners spend more and more on their pets, the demand for pet sitters is expected to rise through 2020. The Bureau of Labor Statistics estimates job growth in the animal care field to be close to 23 percent over the current decade. Pet sitters can often fit their responsibilities in between full-time work, and can take on as many or as few clients as they want. Start-up costs are minimal to none, although certification programs exist.

BEST FOR: Animal lovers with spare time and flexible schedules.

RESOURCES: National Association of Professional Pet Sitters, Pet Sitters International

> **Spotlight On** ... Tara **Heuser,** full-time
> publications coordinator for a trade association
> and part-time pet-sitter; age: 34; location:
> Washington, D.C.

What do you like, and not like, about pet-sitting?

TARA: My apartment doesn't allow pets, so I enjoy getting to spend time with cats and dogs. I also like that I can turn down certain jobs if they conflict with my schedule. My least favorite thing is spending the night at other people's homes, which I tend only to do when watching dogs.

Is it hard to find clients?

TARA: It can be a bit challenging; luckily, word of mouth through my friends has helped tremendously. Three of my current clients are friends of friends. I also place ads on Craigslist occasionally, but that has only led to one client.

Does your pet-sitting income make you feel more secure?

TARA: Yes. It comes in handy over the holidays, since many of my clients travel during that time. I tend to use those earnings to buy presents for family and friends. Especially since I don't make a ton of money at my full-time job, sometimes it's just nice to have a cushion in case of an emergency.

Do you have advice for people who want to get into pet-sitting?

TARA: I would start by talking to friends and asking them to put the word out among their friends and coworkers. I've found that pet owners feel much more comfortable when the person taking care of their pet is recommended from a trusted source. Otherwise, I would advertise in the neighborhood listserv or Craigslist. You want to find out what other pet sitters are charging and keep your rates competitive.

(You can read more about Tara in Chapter 2.)

27. FINE ARTIST

Artists have long pursued their craft alongside full-time employment, simply because it's hard to earn a living on art alone. By taking advantage of proliferating e-commerce sites, from Etsy to RedBubble, artists are finding ways to reach new customers and create additional revenue streams for themselves. Whether they're creating photographs, sculptures, or paintings, there's usually an online market for their creations. Still, finding paying customers isn't easy. The Bureau of Labor Statistics reports that jobs in the field will grow more slowly than average between 2010 and 2020, largely because artwork purchases are a luxury, so sales depend on the economy. According to PayScale.com, the median hourly rate for part-time, self-employed fine artists is just under $20. Expenses consist mainly of art supplies and training.

BEST FOR: Artists who pay the bills through other employment, but who still want to earn money from their creations.

RESOURCES: American Craft Council, Etsy.com, RedBubble.com, Minted.com

28. ONLINE COMMUNITY BUILDER

You won't find "online community builder" included on the Bureau of Labor Statistics' list of jobs, but it's an increasingly popular field for ambitious side-giggers. A mix of journalist, web designer, community organizer, and tech entrepreneur, this job usually exists because someone wants a new way to connect with social or professional circles. Revenues from advertising, partnerships, and lead generation usually come after building a loyal audience; earning potential depends largely on how big an audience the site can attract. Examples include dcurbanmom.com (Chapter 4), NY Creative Interns (Chapter 4), and DailyMuse.com (Chapter 5). A domain name, hosting services, and web design services are among the initial costs, and their prices vary widely. In addition to building the site, online community builders spend a lot of time marketing it and building relationships with potential partners.

BEST FOR: Web savvy, social people who enjoy fostering connections between people.

RESOURCES: Mashable.com, Problogger.net

29. SOFTWARE-SPECIFIC CONSULTANT

Companies, small businesses, and individuals often need help using specific types of software, such as Photoshop, Flash, and Java, and they frequently turn to freelancers to help them. That creates opportunities for anyone with those technical skills. Freelancer.com listed software jobs (related to the programs listed above, along with others) among the fastest growing jobs of 2012. They are also among the best paid, with tech-related consulting work typically bringing in around $70 an hour, according to PayScale.com. The biggest start-up costs are programs they're working on, which many already have on their computers.

BEST FOR: Tech aficionados with the time to take on extra projects.

RESOURCES: Freelancer.com, Elance.com

30. YOGA TEACHER

You don't have to be a yogi yourself to notice the massive explosion in popularity of the ancient practice of yoga. As a result, skilled practitioners can find plenty of opportunities to teach. Given the sporadic hours, yoga teachers often hold down other jobs as well, which are frequently unrelated to what they do on the mat. Part-time, self-employed yoga teachers earn a median hourly rate of just over $25, on par with handymen and writers. Yoga teacher training can be intensive, requiring around 200 hours (or more) of practice and study. Popular classes often take place in the evenings and on weekends, which makes teaching easier to blend with a full-time job.

BEST FOR: Yogis who want to share their love of the practice with other people.

RESOURCES: Kripalu.org, YogaAlliance.org, *Yoga Journal*

31. DISC JOCKEY

Also known as deejays or announcers, disc jockeys can work in radio studios or helm the music booth at events such as weddings. While the Bureau of Labor Statistics projects only modest growth in the field over the current decade, social networking has made it easier for ambitious disc jockeys to brand themselves, find dedicated fans, and earn higher incomes from their craft. Pauly D, from MTV's *Jersey Shore*, exemplifies that possibility. Part-time, self-employed disc jockeys earn a median wage of $35 an hour, according to PayScale.com, which makes the side-gig more lucrative than being a computer repair technician, web developer, or wedding planner. Initial expenses, including high-quality audio equipment, can be high.

BEST FOR: Anyone who loves playing around with beats, mix decks, and popular tunes.

RESOURCES: American Disc Jockey Association, National Association of Mobile Entertainers

32. FLORIST

While the Bureau of Labor Statistics reports that the field of floral arranging as a whole is contracting due to declining interest from consumers, certain sectors, including wedding floral arrangements, continue to grow. The key to finding success is defining your niche and customer base, building a strong online presence, and growing through word of mouth. Florists can also offer tutorials and workshops for customers. About one-third of florists are self-employed; PayScale.com reports that the median pay is $11.40 an hour. Training can include an apprenticeship and certification, but neither is required.

BEST FOR: People with artistic backgrounds who enjoy working with flowers.

RESOURCES: American Institute of Floral Designers, Society of American Florists

Spotlight On ... **Hannah Rohn,** full-time horticulturist at a public garden and part-time, self-employed florist; age: 25; location: Grand Rapids, Michigan

How did you get started?

HANNAH: I was always interested in flowers. I've worked as a landscaper and landscape designer since I was in college, which allowed me to be creative in working with textures, colors, and different plants. That's very different from floral work, but the design principles are the same. I decided to start my own business for one reason—to make more money. My field is very specialized with limited job opportunities, and although I have a top-notch resume with impressive experience, my earning potential is still limited. I knew that floral design would be a fairly easy direction to go initially because of the high markup, minimal overhead, flexible schedule, and, since I'm twenty-five, I'll know a lot of people who will be getting married in the next few years.

What type of training do you have?

HANNAH: As far as hands-on florist experience, I had absolutely none.

How do you combine your floral business with your full-time job as a horticulturist?

HANNAH: It works well because most events that I do for my floral work are on the weekends. So I'm very busy and always working, but my Monday-through-Friday schedule allows me to work special events whenever I want. In theory, in the next two to three years I would get busy enough with weddings to quit my full-time job.

How do you find clients?

HANNAH: At this point, it's largely been word of mouth. You help one friend or family member, and then all of their bridesmaids call, then all of their bridesmaids, and sisters, and roommates, and so on. It's uncanny how busy I've been this year without trying that hard. I also drop off "sample" bouquets at local small businesses, including a wine bar, high-end clothing boutique, and home décor shop when I can, or when I have extras after an event. I drop off the arrangement for no charge, leave a stack of cards, and hope for the best. It's not very aggressive, but at this point I already have about two weddings per weekend, which is a lot. I also made a Facebook page, so people can leave testimonials and images. My full-time job also often leads to guests or volunteers asking if I work on the side as well. They usually want landscaping help, but I also let them know I do flowers.

Do you feel more financially secure because of your side-gig?

HANNAH: Very much. My overhead is essentially nothing, beyond supplies for each event, which I make sure to cover in each client's bill. The nice part about weddings is that they are usually booked far in advance, so financially, I can start to plan a bit more. With landscaping jobs, it's usually much more short term, and you don't know when your next job will be. With weddings, the work is laid out in a contract and I can count on it.

33. HOME ORGANIZER

Thanks to busy, cluttered lives, the field of professional home organizers has grown significantly over the last couple decades. It's also branched into various specializations, including organization for stay-at-home moms, students, or people with certain health issues, including attention-deficit disorder. The job isn't just about sorting through paperwork; organizers help with everything from room design and space management to better organizing the client's time to reach his or her goals. PayScale.com reports that the median hourly rate for part-time, self-employed home organizers is $22.50. Start-up costs are minimal; successful home organizers tend to have appealing websites with useful information for potential clients. Certification is optional.

BEST FOR: People who love spending their weekends sorting through closets and other people's paper piles.

RESOURCES: CertifiedProfessionalOrganizers.org, National Association of Professional Organizers

Spotlight On ... Gillian Carty-Roper,
psychologist and part-time organizer; age: 53;
location: Prince George's County, Maryland

Why did you decide to start organizing on top of your psychology work?
    GILLIAN: I was looking for something with more tangible and immediate outcomes than psychology. I do talk therapy, and

a lot of the time you don't see the changes [in the short run], if ever. That was one of the appeals of organizing work—you can often see the changes sooner. It is very gratifying to help clients use organizing strategies to transform their spaces from cluttered and dysfunctional to supportive.

How did you get started?

GILLIAN: I saw an article about four years ago about an organizer in Maryland, and I called her. She told me about the national organization, and I took some of their classes, including the introduction to professional organization.

Do you use your psychology skills in your organizing work?

GILLIAN: Yes—one of the things I do as a psychologist is develop a treatment plan. That ability to take a problem and then develop a strategy and the steps to help clients get to where they want to go has been very helpful. Also understanding that people don't change until they're ready, and sometimes your view of what a person needs is not what they want, and you have to work toward their vision.

How do you manage your time doing both jobs?

GILLIAN: I recently decided to cut back my psychology work to three days a week, so I can meet with organizing clients on Thursdays, Fridays, and Saturdays.

How do you find your clients?

GILLIAN: I started by sending email to friends and family, and then gave talks at community centers and church groups. I also work with other organizers as an organizer's assistant.

34. SINGER/MUSICIAN

While it's not easy for singers and musicians to market themselves and find paying clients, those who succeed at doing so are richly rewarded: The median hourly wage for part-time, self-employed singers and musicians is around $48—similar to a health care consultant or licensed massage therapist. In addition to live performances, digital recordings and online sales also make it easier for musicians to sell their own music and find new fans. Many performers also earn income by teaching others. After training, which often starts in childhood, the biggest costs are related to marketing to find clients.

BEST FOR: Trained singers or musicians with the time and desire to make money from their skills.

RESOURCES: American Federation of Musicians, CDBaby.com, Freelance Musicians' Association

35. PERSONAL SHOPPER

Personal shoppers have a gift for picking out the perfect outfits for other people. While many work in (and are paid by) department stores, self-employed personal shoppers generally take on clients outside the confines of any single shop. Their clients tend to be financially comfortable, since they're paying for the luxury service, and personal shopping skills often extend into closet organization, design, and styling. Specialties are frequently tied to geography; in areas with large international populations, clients might want help navigating American stores and style, for example. PayScale.com reports that the median hourly rate for self-employed, part-time personal shoppers is $18.50. Training generally comes from life experience and having an eye for style and fit; certifications exist but are not necessary.

BEST FOR: People with enviable taste who enjoy helping others look good.

RESOURCES: Association of Image Consultants International, International Personal Shoppers Association

Spotlight On ... **Alison Lukes,** self-employed wardrobe stylist and personal shopper; age: 35; location: Washington, D.C.

How did you get started?

ALISON: I worked at Michael Kors for four years in the corporate office, handling marketing and brand management. Then I lived in Paris for a year, and decided to move back to Washington, D.C., where I'm from, so I decided to start my business as a way to stay in the fashion industry.

How did you learn the skills to be a stylist and personal shopper?

ALISON: I think it's something you either have or you don't. I did a lot of it at Michael Kors, either on ad shoots or working with celebrities and other clients. I knew I was able to do it well.

How did you get your first clients?

ALISON: I was young enough and naive enough to just start telling people I was doing it. I sent out marketing materials to friends and family, and soon that led to a couple of press articles. It's mostly word of mouth, and just being known as one of the more credible stylists in the area.

Do you work with any particular type of client?

ALISON: I work much more with women than men; men are just about 15 percent of my business. I see a lot of young women who just graduated from college and need to build a professional wardrobe, and new mothers who have maybe been working for ten years and are now at home but still want to look good. I also see a lot of women over fifty who might not be working anymore; their bodies are changing and their needs are changing.

What's your favorite part about the job?

ALISON: Making my clients happy when they feel and look

so much better. It's much more rewarding than I thought it would be.

36. VIDEO EDITOR

Part-time bloggers as well as large corporations rely on freelance video editors, which is why demand is growing for nimble operators. Building an independent side-business as a video editor is also a viable alternative for trained camera operators who are finding their day jobs replaced by new technology, as well as for recent college graduates who want to build their experience while job-hunting. Freelancer. com listed video services as one of its fastest growing fields in early 2012, with over 7,500 job postings on its site. Film and video editors earn a median hourly rate of almost $25, according to PayScale.com. Equipment includes video cameras and editing software, which can be expensive.

BEST FOR: Trained videographers with equipment and connections to local small businesses and other potential clients.

RESOURCES: American Cinema Editors, Elance.com, Freelancer.com

Spotlight On . . . **Mike Harvey,** full-time graduate student in film and electronic media and freelance video editor; age: 46; location: South Arlington, Virginia

How did you get started with video editing?

 MIKE: When I first wanted to get into this business, I volunteered as an assistant editor. I also shot music videos with friends and then on the weekends and at night, went into the editing room and taught myself how to edit, using a book and asking some of the older guys for help. I had permission to use the room and software because I was volunteering. After about a month, I had a music video, and I showed it to my boss. He said, "I'm booking you with clients." That was twenty years ago.

How do you find your clients?

MIKE: Since I've been working in this city for twenty years now, clients usually find me. I used to cold-call people and associations and send them my demo reel or link to my website, or go to networking events and then follow up. Most of the time, I would never hear anything, but there's a little bit that comes from that. A lot of it is recommendations from other editors who I've met over the years. I've learned the power of keeping in touch with clients. During dry times, I'll use freelancing websites.

Were your start-up costs high?

MIKE: Now, anybody can get video editing software for around $300. A laptop, Final Cut Pro, and a hard drive is all you need. With all the extras, it can get up to a few thousand dollars.

What do you like most about video editing?

MIKE: I'm a storyteller, and I'm also very technical. When I was just getting out of college, I was trying to figure out what to do with that. I'm not a writer per se, but I love pictures and organizing a story.

37. BABYSITTER

Parents tend to look for sitters they can trust above any other attribute, including advanced certifications, and jobs often come through word of mouth rather than Internet postings. Still, the growth in popular babysitting websites, such as SitterCity.com, has made it easier for sitters to ramp up their businesses beyond their inner circles. Part-time babysitters earn around $12 an hour, but pay varies widely depending on location. The going rate in many urban areas is $15 and up. Given parents' increasingly hectic work schedules, the Bureau of Labor Statistics projects growth of 20 percent in the field during the current decade. Start-up costs are minimal, although many parents prefer sitters with CPR training and other certifications and will pay more for sitters with other kinds of skills, such as the ability to tutor or cook.

BEST FOR: Caring individuals who love children and are looking to boost their income with night and weekend work.

RESOURCES: SitterCity.com, Care.com

38. CONSTRUCTION WORKER

While most construction workers work full time for companies or small businesses, about one-quarter are self-employed, according to the Bureau of Labor Statistics. The field as a whole is expected to enjoy healthy 25 percent growth between 2010 and 2020, with certain specialties, including brickmasons, carpenters, and pipelayers, seeing even higher levels of growth. Physical strength is a requirement for most construction work, and specialized training, especially in safety or certain trades, can boost your chances of landing gigs. Clients include homeowners, construction companies looking for short-term workers to complete jobs, and small businesses. Construction workers typically earn around $14 an hour, according to government data. General contractors, who plan and manage projects, earn much more, around $45 an hour, according to PayScale.com. Most construction workers learn on the job, although self-employed workers often boost their marketability with certifications, insurance, and licensing.

BEST FOR: People who enjoy physical labor and have had training in a construction-related field, and whose full-time jobs give them the flexibility to show up for short-term, project-based work.

RESOURCES: ConstructionJobs.com, Laborers' International Union of

North America, National Center for Construction Education and Research

39. DANCER/ACTOR/PERFORMER

Performers include street buskers, hoping passersby will drop change—preferably bills—in their hats, as well as stage actors and dancers. Work tends to come in spurts, which is why performers have long held other jobs to support themselves in between gigs. The Bureau of Labor Statistics reports that actors earn around $18 an hour while dancers earn $13 an hour, and job growth in both fields is low to moderate. The ease of sharing online videos, on social networking as well as crowd-funding sites, makes it easier for performers to showcase their skills to potential directors, producers, fans, and funders. Like singers and musicians (#34), many dancers and actors also earn additional income by teaching. Dance instructors earn close to $25 an hour, according to PayScale.com.

BEST FOR: Skilled performers with unrelated day jobs looking to earn money from their craft.

RESOURCES: DanceUSA.org, Kickstarter.com, Screen Actors Guild

40. NUTRITIONIST

Nutritionists help people make better food choices; some specialize in children, weight loss, or specific health issues, such as diabetes or prenatal health. They work for private clients, hospitals, doctor's offices, and nursing homes. Nutritionists typically earn around $26 an hour, according to the Bureau of Labor Statistics, and the demand for their skills is expected to grow over the current decade. The client-based work lends itself to flexibility; about 20 percent work part time and 15 percent are self-employed. Training can be time-consuming: While laws vary by state, most require licenses or certifications, and nutritionists are often also registered dieticians.

BEST FOR: Trained nutritionists looking to pick up extra work and build a private client base.

RESOURCES: American Nutrition Association, American Society for Nutrition, Academy of Nutrition and Dietetics, National Association of Nutrition Professionals

Spotlight On ... Cristin **Wipfler,** self-employed nutritionist; age: 32; location: Middleburg, Virginia

How did you get started?

CRISTIN: I have been interested in nutrition for a long time, but it wasn't offered as a degree where I went to college, and, frankly, I was intimidated by it because it is so heavily based in science and math—two areas where I never had academic confidence. After graduating from college and working for a year in marketing, I decided to go to grad school for public health, which seemed like a happy medium—health without so much science. I loved it. While I was finishing my degree, I was teaching first grade, and over time I realized that nutrition was my passion. I decided to become a registered dietitian, which required me to get a second undergraduate degree in dietetics, complete an internship, and pass a national exam. Every five years, I also need to complete another seventy-five hours of continuing education.

What does your work involve now?

CRISTIN: I started my own practice right after finishing my internship and passing my Registered Dietitian (RD) exam. I work with clients one on one and also give presentations for schools and corporations, consult for businesses, and write articles.

What do you like most about it?

CRISTIN: I love helping people, especially as they stretch and push themselves to reach their health goals and realize their own inner strengths. The world of nutrition is always growing and changing, which adds a fun and challenging aspect to the profession as well. I also really like the flexibility of being my own boss.

How do you find your clients?

CRISTIN: Most of my business so far has been word of mouth. I'm from Middleburg and have worked at one of the schools in town, and my husband works there, too, so a lot of people know me and what I do. I also get referrals from local physicians and therapists. In the future, I hope to build my business by giving more talks in the area, writing articles for the local papers, and other types of outreach.

41. BLOGGER

With the exception of a notable few, bloggers do not generally make much money off of blogs themselves. But they do make money through related activities, including blogging for others (such as companies) or providing content to clients who find them through their blog. Bloggers also earn money by coaching others, selling products such as digital guides or webinars, and teaching workshops. Blogging is easy to do on the side, since writing can be done at any time. The Bureau of Labor Statistics groups bloggers in with writers and authors, who typically earn around $27 an hour. The only equipment required is a computer and Internet connection.

BEST FOR: Writers looking to pick up more work, or people working in nonwriting fields who love to write.

RESOURCES: Blogger.com, ProBlogger.net, Wordpress.com

> **Spotlight On** ... **Carrie Smith,** full-time oil and
> gas accountant, part-time blogger; age: 28; location:
> Dallas, Texas

Why did you decide to start your blog, Careful Cents (carefulcents. com)?

CARRIE: For four years, I worked as a tax specialist, and I heard my clients ask the same type of questions over and over again. I knew I could help more people if I started a blog and built a like-minded community. That's why I created Careful Cents—to create a community of people who can support each other while getting out of debt.

How do you manage blogging with your full-time job?

CARRIE: I keep a detailed schedule for all my projects, writing, and blogging work. That helps me segment what time slots are spent doing what. At the same time, I struck a deal with my boss to work four ten-hour work days instead of five eight-hour ones. Now Fridays and Saturdays are dedicated to my freelance writing and consulting.

Does your blog conflict with your full-time job at all?

CARRIE: Thankfully, I have a very understanding boss and she knows all about my freelance career. She and my other coworkers are very encouraging and enjoy hearing about my latest conference or networking event. Sometimes during my lunch break, I work on my freelance business and blogging, and I feel very blessed to have that flexibility.

How does your blog generate income?

CARRIE: Most of the income I earn through my blog is from my freelance writing contracts, editing, guest-posting, and related writing services. I make a little money from advertising and affiliate sales from products that I use personally and recommend to help others. But the majority of my side-hustle income comes from services like writing. In the future I plan to add some digital products like e-books and guides to my streams of blogging income.

How long did it take you, after launching your blog, to start earning money from it?

CARRIE: It took a good ten months before I started seeing any substantial income from my blog. But I wasn't interested in monetizing at the beginning, so I waited six months before trying to make extra money from my blog. If I started earlier, I could have made more money, but I was more interested in building a solid community.

How did you build up your audience?

CARRIE: I built my audience from scratch and every day I do my best to connect with every single person on a very personal level. If you mention me on Twitter, I'll reply with a quick note or thank you. If you send me an email, I'll always respond. But more than that, I'm truly interested in helping you become more successful, in both life and money. I love seeing and hearing other people's success stories.

42. DATA ENTERER

It might not be the most glamorous of side-gigs, but it's one of the most in demand: In early 2012, Freelancer.com reported that data entry was one of its fastest growing fields, more than doubling over the previous year with over 30,000 job postings listed. That growth is driven by the fact that companies are increasingly outsourcing the work. Related jobs include virtual assistant tasks (such as setting up appointments or organizing email and social media accounts) and data processing. Doing other people's busywork often pays decently (starting at $15 an hour) and can be done at any time of the day or night.

BEST FOR: Strong typists who enjoy working with numbers and spreadsheets.

RESOURCES: Freelancer.com, International Virtual Assistants Association, VirtualAssistantForums.com, Zirtual.com

43. COMEDIAN

In addition to the stand-up kind who performs at clubs and bars, comedians include anyone who earns money off of humor, from joke writers to improvisational actors. Many comedic side-giggers begin because making people laugh is a hobby; they often start getting more serious by joining local groups, taking classes, or performing at open mike nights. Earnings tend to be low and sporadic, but attracting an audience usually generates some revenue, and the side-gig is a popular one among those who love making people laugh. For people who started performing "just for fun," those financial rewards are secondary to the satisfaction that comes from making people laugh.

BEST FOR: Natural hams who want to pick up a few extra bucks on the weekends through their comedic skills.

RESOURCES: National Association of Comedians, local improv groups, World Clown Association

44. COPYWRITING

Copywriters generate text, or copy, for their customers, who tend to be companies looking for help with marketing language, product descriptions, and website language. While they fall under the larger umbrella of writers and authors, copywriters tend to be a more highly paid subset, since they're often working for big companies on campaigns designed to sell services and products. Indeed, senior copywriters are among the most highly paid self-employed, part-time workers according to PayScale.com, typically earning $85 an hour. (Less-senior copywriters earn around $25 an hour.)

BEST FOR: Writers looking for a lucrative income stream to help bankroll their lower-paying creative pursuits.

RESOURCES: Copyblogger.com, Professional Copywriters Association

45. SEARCH ENGINE OPTIMIZATION CONSULTANT

Often referred to simply as "SEO," search engine optimization involves the relatively new and complicated science of improving one's rankings in web searches. Most website owners want to make it as easy as possible for potential customers to find them, which means they want to show up on a web search for related terms. Just how to do that involves studying the tightly guarded and frequently changing logarithms that web search companies such as Google use to generate rankings. Freelancer.com lists over 10,000 SEO-related jobs on its site, with many postings from mid-size companies looking to outsource the task. Hourly rates typically start around $20 an hour and can go up dramatically from there, depending on experience and results.

BEST FOR: Web-savvy marketing professionals looking to pick up extra work with the skills they already have from their day jobs.

RESOURCES: Freelancer.com, Elance.com, Odesk.com

46.
INFORMATION TECHNOLOGY CONSULTANT

Information technology consultants help companies build and manage their computer systems—no small task, especially considering the increasing complexity of those systems. Their responsibilities often range from building networks to managing software upgrades to manning the help desk and ensuring network security. PayScale.com reports that part-time, self-employed IT consultants earn a median wage of almost $70 an hour. On Freelancer.com, almost half of the projects completed by freelancers who also hold full-time jobs fall into the IT, website, or software categories.

BEST FOR: Tech wizards who love playing around on computers.

RESOURCES: Computer World, Freelancer.com

47. TUTOR

Tutors help students on subjects ranging from SAT vocabulary to learning new languages; specialized tutors work with students with learning disabilities or health issues. They generally work for themselves, out of their homes or their students' homes, for educational companies, or in schools. Tutors often hold education degrees as well as certifications and licenses, although self-employed tutors working for families or private schools are not required to hold either. Self-employed, part-time tutors generally earn around $20 an hour, according to PayScale.com. Related fields include college essay editing and college admissions coaching.

BEST FOR: Former or current teachers who enjoy working one on one with students.

RESOURCES: American Tutoring Association, National Tutoring Association, Independent Educational Consultants Association

Spotlight On ... **Hillary Dames,** former teacher and self-employed tutor; age: 33; location: Portland, Oregon

How did you get started as a tutor?

HILLARY: When I was working as a teacher, I tutored students on and off, but my tutoring business began in earnest after having our daughter. When I was on maternity leave, I learned my school district changed my position and, due to budget cuts, reduced my workload. I was not interested in the new position, nor did it seem economically wise to pay for full-time daycare with a part-time teaching salary. I spoke with other teachers who have tutored over the years, and gathered advice and information from them. Then, I let all of my contacts know about my tutoring business, and contacted local schools, put up flyers, passed out business cards, and spoke with friends and acquaintances with school-aged children. After about six weeks, I got my first client, and then word spread quickly and I soon had a nearly-full schedule.

Did you need any special training?

HILLARY: I hold a teaching license and am endorsed to teach pre-K through twelfth grade. I also hold endorsements in language arts, multiple subjects, English as a second language, self-contained classrooms for kindergarten through sixth grade, and reading. The reading specialist endorsement has been very valuable, as the majority of my students are seeking help for literacy-related issues.

What do you like most about it?

HILLARY: I love that I get to set my schedule and spend days with my daughter, and that I'm using my education and tapping into one of my passions—teaching others—to both help clients and help my family financially.

What is the hardest part?

HILLARY: Running a business takes a lot of work and time. Initially, it seemed like there was a lot more rejection than positive feedback. When I don't work, I don't get paid, so I am constantly trying to gather new clients. Part of being a good tutor, after all, is helping students get to the point where they don't need you anymore. Also, it's hard working in the afternoons and evenings, which is when I tutor, since that's when students are available.

48. HOUSEKEEPER

Out of the approximately 1.4 million people who work as housekeepers in the United States, about 12 percent are self-employed. And part-time, self-employed housekeepers earn around $15 an hour, according to PayScale.com. It's not a lot of money for work that is difficult, tiring, and dirty. But the upside is that it's easily scalable, with housekeepers picking up more gigs through word of mouth and their own marketing efforts. Housekeepers can also add various specialties to their services, such as organization (#33) or feng shui, to increase their rates. Writer and former self-employed housecleaner Nancy Peacock describes how she combined her two pursuits in her memoir *A Broom of One's Own* (Harper Perennial, 2008); she finally quit housecleaning when the work became too physically draining.

BEST FOR: People who are physically fit and who don't mind cleaning up after others.

RESOURCES: Association of Residential Cleaning Services, ISSA.com

49. MAKEUP ARTIST

The art of making other people beautiful can be a lucrative one; part-time, self-employed makeup artists earn as much as web developers and interior decorators, or around $31 an hour, PayScale.com reports. While makeup artists who work directly for clients don't generally need certificates or licenses, many makeup artists have them anyway, since salons and spas generally require them and customers often prefer them. Makeup artists also need to know how to market themselves. Related personal-care fields include working as an aesthetician (around $12 an hour), hair dresser or stylist ($15 an hour), and personal shopper (#35).

BEST FOR: Trained makeup artists looking to grow their business and eventually move to self-employment.

RESOURCES: BeautySchools.org, MakeupGeek.com, MakeupMag.com, ProBeauty.org

Spotlight On . . . **Leah McKay,** self-employed makeup artist; age: 47; location: northern Virginia

How did you get started?

LEAH: I was always fascinated with makeup, particularly special effects. During my long teenage rebellion period, I wanted to move to Los Angeles to learn the trade, but didn't have the funds or wherewithal at the time. I ended up training with an aesthetician on the East Coast, and that ended up being the strongest foundation for me to provide the best kind of service. I worked in a salon as an aesthetician doing facials and waxing. Working in a dark room with sounds of the ocean might be conducive to relaxation, but not to a productive, creative mind. I was itching to do more. I became the resident makeup artist at a new Neiman Marcus store in Virginia, and developed my own business on the side, doing makeup for weddings and other clients. Once my side-business grew, I left my job.

How do you find your clients?

LEAH: At first, I called every producer, photographer, and media studio that I could find. I showed up at their door with my portfolio and my makeup, ready to show what I could do and how fast I could do it. It was a period of heavy cold-calling. I knew weddings wouldn't be enough for a full-time business; I needed to supplement during the week, and the television arena was very difficult to break into without any contacts. I got my first break at CNN, and others finally relented and called me in. Once I got in the door, I practiced my work ethic of being completely professional, keeping my commitments, and doing my job. My wedding business also grew, and now, all of my clients come from referrals.

What are your favorite and least favorite parts of the job?

LEAH: My favorite part is the amazing people I meet and get to work with, and helping women feel confident and beautiful. My least favorite part is the early mornings, late nights, and horrendous traffic getting to and from some of my clients.

What's your schedule like now?

LEAH: Weddings are my priority, so I work every weekend, often on Sunday. It's hard to say no sometimes, and have a break when I need one. I often work seven days a week, although the days vary from two hours of work to ten or eleven hours. Balance is crucial for my physical and mental well-being, so I've learned to finesse my schedule around my own needs, as well as those of my clients.

50. WEDDING OFFICIANT

The number of self-employed, freelancing wedding officiants is grow-ing, as more couples opt for customized ceremonies that fall outside of religious traditions. Becoming an ordained minister online is easy, through organizations such as the Universal Life Church. (Specific state requirements for marriage licenses vary.) The pay also varies by geographic region and type of wedding, but officiants typically earn $200 and up for their services per ceremony, along with reimburse-ment for any travel costs. Since the work generally takes place on eve-nings and weekends, it's an easy gig to combine with almost any full-time job.

BEST FOR: Strong public speakers who enjoy working with couples to create meaningful ceremonies.

RESOURCES: firstnationministry.org, ulcweddingofficiants.com, wed-dingministers.com

Spotlight On . . . **Yvonne Doerre**, full-time social worker and part-time wedding officiant; age: 43; location: Washington, D.C.

How did you get started?

YVONNE: My best friend was getting married, and she and her fiancé weren't religious. We started talking about how Joey on *Friends* performed Monica and Chandler's wedding. I went online and found there was nothing to it—I registered at the Universal Life Church; it took fifteen minutes and was free. I've since learned that the legality of the wedding itself is all jurisdiction-depen-dent; D.C. required me to register and sent me a certificate.

Did you have some kind of training that gave you the skills to lead a marriage ceremony?

YVONNE: I did improv theater for six years; I'm naturally comfortable in front of people. For my first one, I was so nervous, and it went really well. With my background as a clinical social worker, I've done some family therapy, and the pre-wedding meeting with the couple is very much related to social work. . . . My work often involves thinking about relationships, helping people navigate relationships, and thinking about what's important. I've thought about expanding my services to include three premarital counseling sessions and then one session six months after the wedding. That social work element is why I enjoy it and why I'm decent at it—I'm asking people about their relationship and they're reflecting on it. I hope that brings an element of depth to it, and it's not just someone saying words.

Does being an officiant contribute to your overall financial security?

YVONNE: It could, if I grew my business more. I've varied the charges but gone up to $500. I'd love to do one a month, and maybe bring in $6,000 a year.

Note: Yvonne served as the author's wedding officiant.

Star Side-Giggers

HERE'S HOW YOU CAN FIND MOST OF THE SIDE-GIGGERS MENTIONED in this book, listed alphabetically:

NAME	FULL-TIME JOB	SIDE-GIG	WHERE TO FIND THEM	PAGE NUMBER
Meredith Alexander	stay-at-home mom	nonprofit founder	milkandbookies.org	133
Jessi Baden-Campbell	coordinating producer	opera singer	jessibaden.com	87
Emily Beach	field hockey coach	inventor	dribbledr.com	21
Jenny Blake	career developer	life coach/author	lifeaftercollege.org	40
Joe Cain	police captain*	tax preparer	finestfinancialgroup.com	5
Michael Carvin	private equity analyst*	website creator	smartasset.com	140
Martin Cody	medical sales	online wine seller	cellarangels.com	101
Nicole Crimaldi	social media manager	career blogger	mscareergirl.com	7
Peter Davis	college student*	website creator	commonplaceusa.com	78

NAME	FULL-TIME JOB	SIDE-GIG	WHERE TO FIND THEM	PAGE NUMBER
Corinne Delaney	graphic designer	classical singer	corinne-delaney.com	99
Prakash Dheeriya	professor	author	finance4kidz.com	143
Chris Furin	deli employee*	cake designer	cakesbychrisfurin.com	1
Katy Gathright	college student*	website creator	designedgood.com	67
Tara Gentile	bookstore clerk*	blogger/coach	taragentile.com	6
Alexis Grant	reporter*	digital entrepreneur	alexisgrant.com	125
Chris Hardy	instrument repairer	voiceover artist	chrishardyworld.com	17
Mike Harvey	graduate student	video editor	sharpypictures.com	211
Todd Henry	creative director*	author/speaker	accidentalcreative.com	25
Febe Hernandez	federal worker	jewelry designer	designsbyfebe.com	32
Maia Heyck-Merlin	senior advisor	organization guru	brasstackstime.com	20
Morgan Hoth	teacher*	silk scarf designer	morgansilkscarf.com	44
Nicholas Ignacio	college student	lawn care company founder	strongstudentslawncare.com	96
Tory Johnson	journalist	entrepreneur	womenforhire.com	8
Emily Kaminski	stay-at-home mom	website creator	frugalpharmacies.com	127
Beena Katekar and Sudhansu Samal	IT workers	app developers	thesqube.com	16
Calee Lee	videographer	book publisher	xistpublishing.com	33
Jason Malinak	accountant	Etsy seller	etsy.com/shop/JJMFinance	31
Melissa McCreery	consultant*	website creator	thedailymuse.com	72
Emily Miethner	community manager*	organization creator	nycreativeinterns.com	56

NAME	FULL-TIME JOB	SIDE-GIG	WHERE TO FIND THEM	PAGE NUMBER
Douglas Lee Miller	social media manager	social media coach	dbmill.com	35
Jeffrey Nash	salesman	inventor	thejuppy.com	91
Lisa Nelson	illustrator/ designer*	freelance illustrator	mylittlebuffalo.com	66
Jason Nicholas	veterinarian	vet safety advocate	thepreventivevet.com	129
Kylie Ofiu	hairdresser	blogger/author	kylieofiu.com	24
April Bowles Olin	therapist*	creative entrepreneur	blacksburgbelle.com	62
Sydney Owen	marketer	career coach	sydneyowen.com	46
Ben Popken	reporter	improv comedian	iambenpopken.com	115
Erica Sara	merchandiser*	jewelry designer	ericasaradesigns.com	51
Carrie Smith	accountant	blogger	carefulcents.com	217
Maria Sokurashvili	IT specialist*	website creator	dcurbanmom.com	54
Amy Stringer-Mowat	architect*	Etsy seller	aheirloom.com	83
Jennifer Teates	law firm manager	money writer	twitter.com/jennyswave25	90
Stephanie Theodore	department manager	art studio owner	theodoreart.com	100
AJ Thomas	program manager	nonprofit founder	infuseprogram.org	132
John Tullock	community manager*	gardener	johntullock.blogspot.com	123
Ebony Utley	professor	speaker and writer	theutleyexperience.com	93
Tracey Webb	grant writer	nonprofit founder	blackbenefactors.org	134
Mark Wilson	technology writer	website creator	philanthroper.com	128
Dana Lisa Young	content manager	holistic healer	dragonflyreiki.net	102

* An asterisk indicates that the side-gigger no longer holds a full-time position.

APPENDIX
C

Five Common Pitfalls to Avoid

1. Waiting until you're "ready" to launch. Many side-giggers in this book discovered their side-gigs almost by accident; a friend asked them for a favor, and suddenly they were in the floral business, or running a social marketing consultancy, or pet-sitting. Instead of slowing down and first building a Facebook page or stocking up on inventory, they said "yes" to the opportunity in front of them, and their side-gigs grew from there.

2. Letting the first failure stop your progress. Almost all of the side-giggers interviewed in this book experienced some kind of setback or hiccup early on, and in fact, many still experience occasional failures: a pitch gets rejected, a client gives negative feedback, or a new digital product flops. But they keep going, because they know that one rejection doesn't mean their contributions are worthless. Instead, they take it as proof that they are trying something new and taking risks, some of which are bound to fail.

3. Thinking you're earning too little to make a difference. Many side-giggers make what seems like small amounts of cash on a weekly or monthly basis: $100 to $200 a month, or just a few thousand dollars a year. But not only does that money add up over time—$3,000 a year equals around $40,000 after ten years if it's in an account earning 5 percent interest—it also represents new possibilities in the event of a layoff. An income of $200 a month, earned from working a few hours a week, can often be scaled up dramatically if time allows. Even small side-gigs represent new opportunities and potential.

4. Overinvesting in start-up costs. It's easy to plow savings into a side-gig before it's even launched: a beautiful website, a professional marketing plan, trips to conferences and new certifications. But before investing a cent, successful side-giggers often first look for ways to bring in revenue to offset those costs, while simultaneously testing the market. That might mean offering nutrition consulting services before setting up a new website, or selling an e-book through Amazon or another existing e-commerce channel before printing paperback versions.

5. Working too hard for too little. When side-giggers are first starting out, they sometimes make the mistake of undercharging for their services, or setting up a business model that would require a 100-hour-a-week schedule to earn a living wage. A classic example is selling a handcrafted crocheted sweater for the same price as a store-bought, machine-produced one. Indeed, simply charging more for products and services can signal quality to potential buyers. Testing the market to see what it can bear, and checking out competitors' prices, can help side-giggers avoid starting too low.

Index

ABOUT THE AUTHOR

Kimberly Palmer is the senior money editor and Alpha Consumer blogger at *U.S. News & World Report* and author of *Generation Earn: The Young Professional's Guide to Spending, Investing, and Giving Back* (Ten Speed Press). She has appeared on NBC's *Today Show*, CNBC, CNN, and local television and radio shows across the country to talk about making smart money decisions. She has also written for the *Washington Post*, the *Wall Street Journal*, and the *Asahi Shimbun/International Herald Tribune* in Tokyo as a Henry Luce Scholar. She holds a master's degree in public policy from the University of Chicago and a bachelor's degree in history from Amherst College. Kimberly lives in the Washington, D.C., area with her husband and their two children. You can connect with her online at bykimberlypalmer.com.